Downsizing

Homes

Downsizing Homes

What You Need To Know

Ricki Eichler McCallum

Copyright © 2020 Ricki Eichler McCallum

Original Edition
March 25, 2020

ALL RIGHTS RESERVED

No part of this book may be reproduced or transmitted in any form or by any means; electronic or mechanical including photocopying, recording, or by any information storage and retrieval system without permission in writing from the Author.

The author and publisher have made every effort to ensure the information in this book is accurate as of press time. The author and publisher hereby disclaim and do not assume liability for any loss, injury, damage, or disruption caused by errors or omissions, regardless of whether any errors or omissions result from negligence, accident, or any other cause. Readers are encouraged to verify any information contained in this book prior to taking any action on the information.

CastNet Press
P. O. Box 213
West Branch, MI 48661

ISBN 9798623873293

Printed in the United States of America

Also by Ricki Eichler McCallum

Finally A Broker!
Open Your Own Real Estate Office

DEDICATION

Dedicated to those who believe that home ownership is the way to health, happiness, and prosperity.

PREFACE

There comes a time when we suddenly awaken from the dream that has been our life. We look in the mirror and don't recognize the old man or woman looking back at us.

The changes came about so slowly; we did not even notice the wrinkles appearing. Our hair has turned gray or fallen out for the most part. Our posture is not so straight anymore. It hurts just to get up from our reclining chair. Who is this person, we ask ourselves. Is that really me?

"Where has the time gone? It was just yesterday we were so young, just starting out in life. I remember when we bought our first house," you might say to your spouse.

He reminds you how many homes you have owned in the past. The first one was small. Then the second one, a little larger to accommodate your family's growing needs. The third one was nicer as the income increased. The fourth and so on met your needs as your family grew and then out grew your homes. Recreational opportunities and conveniences played a part in every move. Job transfers lead to moves as well.

Now, the time has come for downsizing. The children are gone. The grandchildren are growing up fast. They barely have time for the old folks anymore, and the old folks' needs have changed. Yes, we've become the "Old Folks".

The memories and emotions can be overwhelming and paralyzing when thinking of moving. Don't let these obstacles stand in your way. A new home or lifestyle can add new memories and happiness. There are lots of alternatives that did not exist just a few years ago. In this book, we will look at many of these options. Maybe one will be right for you.

There are many decisions to make. The first decision is to sell your home and downsize to a smaller home that is more easily maintained. Timing is important with this decision. Another is to give away, sell or donate excess furnishings, personal items, collections and more. How do you begin? This book will answer many of your questions and help you get started.

Ricki Eichler McCallum has been a real estate broker for the past forty years. She is a REALTOR®, a member of local, State and National Associations of REALTORS®. She has extensive knowledge and experience working with seniors. Her office in Kerrville, Texas, dealt primarily with seniors. Kerrville is a retirement haven. The average age for newcomers to the area is over age 55.

Seniors face many obstacles, but downsizing and preparing to buy a retirement home is easier when you know what to look for and what to watch out for. This book answers many of those questions and can help in the transition to the next chapter in your life. Moving can be fun and exciting. Much of the stress can be removed by better understanding the processes and options before you begin. This book will help make your next move smooth and painless.

Ricki Eichler McCallum

Broker, ABR, GRI, e-PRO, TAHS

Table Of Contents

Chapter 1	Reasons for Downsizing	15
Chapter 2	Generations	27
Chapter 3	What Kind of Home Is Best For You?	43
Chapter 4	What to Look For When Buying	57
Chapter 5	Taxes and Insurance	75
Chapter 6	Reverse Mortgages and Other Loans	83
Chapter 7	Buying vs. Renting	103

Chapter 8	Safety First	111
Chapter 9	Furnishings and Treasures	121
	What To Do With Them	
Chapter 10	How to Choose the Right Agent	133
Chapter 11	Are You Ready To Make The Move?	149

Chapter 1

Reasons for Downsizing

There are many reasons for downsizing, but the most common one has to do with getting older. Children have grown up and moved away, and you no longer need such a large home. The extra expense in upkeep for a larger home may not be worth it to you anymore. Extra expense for taxes and insurance can also be a factor. Money is the biggest concern. You don't want to run out of money in retirement. So, saving as much as you can is important.

As we age, we must consider the work it takes to maintain our homes. Cleaning a larger home can be too much work if you have health problems. The lawn and landscaping is a major concern too. Repairs or heavy maintenance is best done by younger people. You have to protect your health in retirement. Over exertion has been known to cause heart attacks, and even a simple fall can impair you for life.

If you have plenty of money to hire someone to perform these tasks, that's different. Most seniors, however, must watch their expenses carefully. Seniors worry about having enough money to live comfortably throughout retirement. So cutting extra expenses is easiest by downsizing.

When is it Time to Downsize? How will you know it is time?

Only you can answer this question. The size of your home, the yard, the cleaning, the maintenance, the extra expense, these are all good reasons for downsizing. The questions and answers in this book will help you to know when the time is right for you.

To be comfortable in selling your larger home and moving to a smaller one, you must rid yourself of many of your possessions. This is a good time to share your valuables or special treasures with loved ones. This is the hardest thing to do when downsizing. Giving up special articles that hold emotional value to you but may not hold the same value to the person you are planning to give it to. Don't expect others to feel the same way about your things or you may get your feelings hurt.

It is best to inventory your things. Make lists. Do you have collectibles? You will want to give them as a complete set, most likely. Going through your things and deciding what you want to keep and what you want to give away is an enormous job. It can take quite a bit of time.

Some of your things can be packed away and stored for giving away at a later date. You may even want to sell some things. This could bring in some extra cash. There are people who can help you do all these things. A quick search on the internet will give you a list of names. Estate sellers, REALTORS®, Organizers, Movers, can answer questions and some may know other people in your area that you can hire to help.

Don't forget to ask friends and neighbors if they know of anyone that could also help. Hiring someone that is licensed or bonded is best. They are coming into your home and working with your valuables. Remember, safety first.

Saving Money and Lowering Maintenance are now your priorities. After you complete your inventory and decide on what to keep and what not to keep, you can decide what size home will be best for you. Moving into the right size home is important. If it is too large, it is a waste of money. If it is too small, it is not comfortable. So choose the right size.

Is It Time To Downsize?

Your current home may have extra bedrooms that are not being used for bedrooms anymore because the children or grandchildren have grown up and are gone from your home. If you can repurpose these rooms for an office or a second living area, these rooms might not be considered wasted space. Many people are afraid to turn bedrooms into different use rooms because of company they may have in the future. Hide-a-bed sofas and murphy beds or even blow up air mattresses can take care of the occasional company that needs to spend the night.

Consider how often you use a room and then consider the extra cost that room is bringing to your monthly budget. This is one of the easiest ways to save money and get more use out of your home's square footage.

Repurpose your space. Be creative. Now that you've done this, is your home still too large for your retirement needs? If so, let's look at downsizing, selling your current home and buying a smaller place.

Let's think of your living space. Is your living room filled with articles of furniture you really don't need? Does anyone need seating for eight to ten people? Or would seating for four or five be enough? Are there extra end tables or lamps or desks that are not being used? There are usually many things in the living area that you do not need for comfortable living.

We accumulate many things during our lifetimes. We have souvenirs from places we have visited. Some of these "souvenirs" are quite large. I have a water vase that stands over three feet tall in my living area right now. It is from Turkey and is a "souvenir" from when my husband was stationed there many years ago in the military. Is it something I could give away and make more room? Probably. If I were moving to a smaller home with half the living area, it would be first on my list.

So, go through your rooms and look with the eyes of a stranger. A stranger will have no sentiments for your personal belongings. If your belongings don't fulfil a necessary purpose for day to day living, they are things that can be parted with. There are exceptions, however. My exceptions are things that hold too strong an emotion. Things my children gave me or made for me that cannot be replaced. Photos, of course, are in this list. However, I currently have nine big plastic boxes of loose pictures. I cannot keep all these. So, I am in the process of separating them and I will give most of them to my grandchildren shortly.

Giving some of your things to the children or grandchildren while you are here is much better than waiting until you are gone. You get to enjoy seeing them respond to your gifts. You may get to share some special times reminiscing about photos or material objects you pass down to them. There are many rewards in giving to them now rather than waiting. It also helps you to downsize. It's a win-win.

Now, let's look at the kitchen. The kitchen you have always dreamed of may currently be in your possession. How do you begin to downsize here? Many don't cook anymore, or not as much as they once did.

When you have a large family, it seems you are cooking all the time. When it is just you or you and your spouse, the cooking will lessen. Once, you had lots of company and made big meals. Do you still do that?

My kitchen has all the utensils, pots, pans, electric appliances, linens, dishes, glassware, everything imaginable. I love to cook, but as the years have gone by, my energy is not what it once was. I think about preparing a large meal; the prep, the cooking, the serving and then the clean-up. That's a lot of work. So, a sandwich or a salad makes its way to the table and the thought of a big meal goes away.

Does this happen to you? If so, it may be time to look at downsizing that big kitchen and trading it in for a galley kitchen that requires fewer steps while cooking and cleaning. Just make sure your new kitchen has room for a wheelchair if you might ever need one. If those electric appliances are just sitting on your counters and not getting regular use, you may not need them at all.

We have already discussed the use of bedrooms that receive little use. Turn those rooms into a more useful room like a study, office, den, hobby room, exercise room, or whatever you fancy. Don't let that space go unused. When you no longer need so many rooms, is it time for you to downsize?

Bathrooms, are they ever too big? I would have trouble saying yes to that question. However, as we get older, our needs in the bathroom change also. Grab bars around the tub and the toilet are often necessary. Walk-in showers are easier for older adults if the step up is not too high, but a tub is sometimes nice for our occasional aches and pains. A hot bath can relieve minor pains but often times we only use showers because it is too hard to get in and out of a tub. So adding a walk-in tub can be an expense well worth its cost.

The walk-in tubs today have large doors that seal, making it easy to enter and exit. Some tubs have heated seats for added comfort. Buying one that has the quick drainage is best. Seniors love these tubs because they are easy to use and so relaxing.

I had a friend recently that broke his ankle and leg. He is very fit and active but this accident impaired his ability to get into the shower. The shower was large but the lip was just a few inches too high for my friend to navigate. These are things we should remember when we are looking for a new home or remodeling our current home. Those few inches made it impossible for him to get into the shower.

A well-designed bathroom will have enough space for a wheelchair to enter and exit. If your current home's bathroom does not fit these needs, it is time to think about downsizing?

Do you have two or more living areas? Do you have other rooms you don't really need? Is your home so large, you take more than a whole day just to clean it? Is it time to downsize?

Let's consider the lawn and the landscaping? For me, I love to garden. It helps to keep me active and in good health. I enjoy digging in the dirt and planting flowers and vegetables.

I bend over and I walk and I lift heavy things while gardening. It's good for me, but afterwards I have lots of aches and pains from over exertion. This is good exercise and can help keep us young, but there comes a time when we have too much space for lawn, landscaping and gardening.

When it becomes a chore or more than we can do in a reasonable amount of time, maybe it is time to downsize. Hiring work done around the house can be expensive. If we have unlimited income, that is all right. If we do not, it may be time to downsize.

When is the time right to downsize? It is different for everyone. If people are telling you to consider downsizing, maybe you should listen to them. We try to hold on to what is familiar as long as we can. I have seen older people stay in their homes too long without downsizing. It can take a toll on a person. Moving can be fun and exciting, not depressing as some may think. A new home may be just what you need to become more active. It can be a relief to have a smaller place that is easier to take care of and maintain.

If we don't need the extra space, and if the maintenance and cleaning is more than we can do comfortably, those are two good reasons to downsize. Now let's look at the best reason for downsizing, the money we can save!

We will start with taxes. Taxes are based on the assessed value of your home. Many times, the tax assessor-collector bases the value on square footage. So, if you have more square footage than you need, you are possibly paying more taxes than you need to pay.

Home owner's insurance is priced on square footage as well. So, your insurance may be higher than necessary if you have more square footage than you need. Lowering taxes and insurance is important for anyone, but especially for seniors. Seniors often live on fixed incomes. Lowering taxes and insurance can make life better.

Saving money on taxes and insurance is great, but let's also consider the utility bills. Heating and air conditioning rooms you no longer use is a waste of money. You can shut off vents to those rooms, but not having those rooms to clean and maintain is easier. How much money have you spent on cleaning, on painting, maybe floor covering, or plumbing repairs for a room you could virtually do without? There are lots of ways to save money and when we retire that is important.

Downsizing by selling your current home and buying a smaller, less expensive home can put some money in the bank for you. This is great for seniors living on a fixed income. An additional nest egg comes in handy in the latter years.

Downsizing requires lots of thought and research. Have a REALTOR® come look at your current home and give you a market analysis of what your home could bring. Find out what a smaller home in your area or maybe another area would cost. Do some research to see if downsizing is what you need and if this is the best time for you to downsize. Market conditions are very important to consider.

If there is no monetary benefit because of the current market conditions, it might not be a good time for you to downsize. However, if the reasons to downsize have more to do with maintenance or ease of living, it may be time even if the monetary value is not there.

I have shared some questions with you that will make it easier for you to know when the time has come to sell. In the following chapters, you will look at various home types and lifestyles to decide which option is best for you. You will learn what to look for when purchasing your new home. I discuss ways to purchase when cash is tight, available loan programs, and various ways to save money. We look at the advantages of buying versus renting, safety, what to do with furnishings, how to choose the right agent and making the move.

So, is it time for you to downsize?

Chapter 2

Generations

Who are the Silent Generation? Who are the Baby Boomers? Who are Generation X? What about Generation Y, the Millennials? Every generation will define themselves by certain principles or events in the lives of its people. How does the generation you are a part of affect your retirement and downsizing issues?

In this chapter, we will divide these generations and look at specific characteristics and needs of each. Of course, some things will overlap. Needs are different for each person depending on activity levels, geographical areas, family ties, and so much more. Read on and see in which group you identify.

The Silent Generation consists of people born between 1925 and 1944. Some of these people grew up during war and depressed times. They are considered hardworking, have strong will power, are loyal, respect authority and live by the old saying "waste not, want not."

There are roughly 20 million adults in this category in their late 70s thru 90s. The term "Silent Generation" came from "Children are to be seen and not heard". Some people put the stopping point at 1942 and others at 1944.

These people grew up in a time when humility was valued and the expected norm was dignity and modesty. They have strong work ethics. They usually are prudent savers. Personal responsibility and faithful commitments mean a lot to these folks. If you are a REALTOR®, trying to sell a home to a person like this, your job is much easier. You can expect your client to have the funds necessary to buy or a good credit rating to obtain a loan usually, since they are proven savers. Their younger years taught them the importance of saving money. Being reared in this time period had a long lasting impact on people's lives.

If you are a REALTOR® and trying to help sell a person's home from this generation, you can expect their word to be their bond. I loved working with people in this age group. I did not worry so much about them not telling me the truth, and it made my job as their real estate agent much easier.

I knew they would sometimes take their time deciding, but once made, they would follow through with that decision. Many younger people could learn wiser ways by following in their grandparents' shoes.

The Silent Generation is an age group that requires a little more assistance in the home and less maintenance. So, they will look for grab bars in the baths, room for wheelchairs, one-story homes, and locations near shopping and medical facilities and possible transportation options. These are the most important things the silent generation will be looking for in their new homes. We will discuss other special details in a later chapter on what to look for when buying your new home.

I cannot stress enough the **importance of location** for this generation. Medical facilities and shopping are most important. Transportation needs to be considered as well. Many counties have transportation available with just a phone call. If you are in the right location with everything convenient, it can mean staying independent longer. So make location a priority.

If you are moving to a new town, city or state, check out the medical facilities before you buy. If you cannot get good doctors or your insurance will not pay in the new area, find another place.

Once I had a client move from Florida to Texas. They loved the area and their new home. However, after they bought they checked out their insurance and it would not transfer to Texas facilities. It was a special insurance they had and they needed it for their particular health problems. They decided after only a year, to move back to Florida. It was for health insurance reasons. So, please check before you make the move. It was costly for this couple and so sad.

Being able to go shopping or out to eat makes life much more enjoyable. If you are located in an area where you can still drive because the traffic is not so heavy, you can go where you want. Heavy traffic areas are not good for seniors. Therefore, I put **location as number one** when looking for your new home.

Number two has to be **one-story homes**. Stairs are difficult to navigate with just a little arthritis. Try navigating them after a surgery; it does not work.

If you have stairs, there is the possibility of installing a stair lift or elevator. The stair lifts available today are not that expensive and work well. They take up a lot of room on the stairs and make it difficult just to walk up most staircases. When you get ready to sell this home, be advised you may need to remove this before selling. I have had homes listed with stair lifts on the market for a long time, and they do not sell well. While you are living there, however, it can be the answer to your needs.

Sometimes an elevator can be installed. It could cost quite a bit, however, and maintaining it will also come with a price. If you have a choice between homes with stairs and homes without stairs, choose wisely.

Number three is the bathroom. Is it large enough to bring in a wheelchair if needed? Are there grab bars around the tub and the toilet, or is there room to install them? These are so important. They can save you from a fall.

Lots of people need wheel chairs from time to time. *My son was a young man when he got sick and needed a wheelchair.* Getting from one room to the next is important, but the bathroom is a necessity. Measure the doors and the space by the counter if you might need to get a wheelchair through the space.

Number four is the kitchen. Just like the bathroom, the kitchen should be able to accommodate a wheelchair. Galley kitchens are long and narrow. Some will work great, but others are too narrow and make turning a wheelchair impossible. This is not the kind of kitchen you need. Make sure the home will work for you now and in the future.

My friend, Nancy, is part of the Silent Generation and has just recently moved to another state to be near her grandchildren. She thought she would never make such a move, but considering a very cold winter last year, she decided it would be worth the move to be in a warmer location this winter. She is very happy with her decision to move.

I asked Nancy what advice she would give others that wish to downsize. Her advice is to do it as soon as you retire and try not to accumulate so much. She said downsizing is the smartest move you can make. It will reduce stress.

The Silent Generation is a group of people we owe a lot to for their contributions to our society. They deserve a special place to call home in their later years. Hopefully, all will learn from this book what to look for when purchasing that special home for retirement years.

*****

Baby Boomers are a group of people born in the years 1945 through 1964. This time period encompasses the end of World War II, the Korean War, and the Vietnam War.

During this time period, 76 million Americans were born. Just the sheer number of births makes the baby boomers an unusual generation. It was largely a post-war time, and business exceeded expectations during this era. The vast improvement in the economy led to more spendable income for average Americans. The baby boomers had more luxuries; more food, clothing, cars, and education than previous generations. Even though most baby boomers passed on their parents' values, this excess wealth led to cultural changes that are still seen today.

This was good news for the real estate market. Baby boomers took advantage of air transportation, new technology and more which enabled them to transfer from job to job all across the country. This meant buying and selling homes throughout their careers.

Any REALTOR® will tell you, the easiest way to make money is to invest in real estate. So, just the average family making several moves during their careers could increase their wealth sizably. Many do. With the economy growing so rapidly in the last half of the twentieth century, many baby boomers have become millionaires.

Others, however, have led a life of excess and spent most of their earned income. Statistics show that one third of baby boomers have no money saved for retirement. Life could change for many baby boomers as they retire on social security alone.

If these people own their homes, they will be able to use the equity built up for retirement. If they do not own their own homes, life could become quite hard for them. We will discuss loans and reverse mortgages in a later chapter. This could be an answer for many with housing needs.

During the years 2010-2030, one in five Americans will be over the age of 65. This will mean a strain on Medicare and other governmental programs.

If you are a baby boomer and looking to downsize your larger home and get into a smaller home that is easier to maintain, you need to understand you are not alone. One in five of your neighbors are doing the same thing.

What impact will this have on you? It could make housing prices higher when buying a new home. The more demand there is, the higher the price. Retirement communities will be in big demand.

It could also benefit you, as builders will be looking at the changing lifestyles of so many Americans. Building new communities for seniors and smaller homes for a large segment of the population could mean more options for you, the buyer.

Today's housing market offers seniors many choices. We will look at all these options in future chapters.

I have a friend that recently moved across country to be near her daughter. Denise is a Baby Boomer like me. Denise is a saver and knew she could make the move financially if she so desired. Her reluctance was in moving her 87- year- old mother. She was not sure her mother could make the move or would want to make a move so far from her longtime home. Denise and her mom lived in separate houses in separate towns nearby. Denise had promised herself never to bring up the subject of moving.

One day out of the clear blue, her mom said she could not take another cold winter. Denise knew the time was right. Where to start? How to begin? The thought of retiring from work, selling her house, selling furniture, packing herself and her mom, selling her mom's car, arranging for doctors in the new place; it all seemed overwhelming. The new place was over a thousand miles away, and this added to the burdensome tasks.

For Denise and her mom, there was only one thing to do. Seek answers from God. They went to Him in prayer and suddenly things began to happen. They called some friends to come pray about their move and discussions led to her mom's car being sold. A few days later, her daughter called about a condo in the new location that would be perfect for both of them. After many photos and telephone calls, the condo was theirs. Her daughter was eager to help get it ready for move in. Denise called a REALTOR®, listed her house for sale one afternoon. That very night, the first showing occurred. The widow lady buyer sat down in Denise's recliner and began to cry. She told Denise, "This is the house I have been looking for." The home sold for cash and closed within a month.

Garage sales and auctions took care of furniture and household goods. Denise and her mom only kept what they could not part with. Sentimental pieces and family heirlooms that were not given away, along with personal items, were the only things packed in the pod that was delivered to their new place.

Doctors' appointments were kept and new doctors were searched for in the new location. To their surprise, Denise's mother's former eye doctor from ten years ago now lives in the new place Denise and her Mom call home. So, there was a happy reunion. Denise says, "God took care of everything, including providing doctors we already knew and loved."

I asked Denise had she planned her steps ahead of time because I knew she had entertained the idea of moving for several years. She said she never planned one step. It was all God helping her.

Retirement came and goodbyes were said. Denise and her Mom left lots of good friends but moved closer to family. They are the kind of people who will be dearly missed and the kind that will have new friends right away.

I asked Denise for her advice to others desiring to downsize and move. She replied, "Do not be afraid to step out. It's a faith thing. Depend on the Lord for your answers." She told me about a saying she heard years ago and remembered. It was something like "God has the pen, He is writing your story. Don't try to take the pen away from Him." She did not know who said this, but it meant a lot to her.

She never thought her mom would want to move, but now only two months after the first conversation, she is living carefree, a thousand miles away. It can be done, sometimes easier than you think.

Today's Baby Boomers will experience health issues in coming years and consideration of all these things and downsizing will help you decide on future home purchases. Baby Boomers have been the largest population for a long time. However, in 2019, Generation X overtook this generation with a population of approximately 88.5 million people.

*****

Generation X are people born between 1965 and 1979. They are rapidly becoming the next generation of retirees having reached the AARP standard for senior, age 50 and over.

Generation X experienced the 80s, a cultural time of transition, a time when divorce was common and single-parent households were not rare. Latchkey kids are a term given many because these children often came home to empty houses as parents were working. This generation has had different problems to overcome than previous generations. A lack of social or family ties is often associated with this generation. A new independence has also been seen in this generation.

As a by-product of this independence and confidence, many have become entrepreneurs. This can do spirit developed by cultural influences has led many to rewarding careers. Owning one's own business is much more a reality in this generation than in the two previous generations when most people worked for large companies and stayed with one company their entire lives. These people often stayed with a company because of the retirement programs that were offered.

Generation X people are more apt to try new things and embrace technology than Baby Boomers. This generation has been open to the new computerized world and in a position of strength to build companies with the birth of new technologies.

According to governmental reports, many people become handicapped and unable to work in their 50s. This means many of the Generation X population could begin to downsize and look for smaller homes as well.

As with Baby Boomers, Generation X has a large segment of their population that is not prepared for retirement. The retirement programs of large corporations that so many Baby Boomers relied on years before are no longer there. Savings and investments are easier to put off when you work for yourself. Therefore, many are left unprepared for retirement.

The housing market in America today is doing well, and the inventory is small. Builders have not kept pace with demand since the Recession of 2008. Home prices are experiencing a boost and most markets are seller's markets. Homes do not stay on the market very long at all, if they are priced right and in good condition.

If you are considering downsizing and making a smaller home purchase, research your market carefully. Consider less expensive market areas, if that is an option. Most young adults who live in rural areas or small towns move into larger cities as they reach adulthood. That's where they find the most jobs. When retirement time comes, jobs are not a consideration. Why not consider moving back to a rural area or small town? The cost of living is sometimes much less because housing prices are less. Many retirees find living in a smaller town a good thing. Convenience and less traffic are two big things that retirees love most about living in smaller areas. Lots of retirees move south where it is warmer, but not all. Better home prices can sometimes be found in colder areas. So, don't discount looking in the north as well as the south.

Watch the interest rates and make your move at the most advantageous time for you. One percentage point difference in your rate can mean a lot in your monthly payments and in the kind of home you may be able to afford. Preparing in advance always has advantages, if you have the option. Start planning now for retirement. It is never too early.

I know of people who have bought their retirement home many years before they would need it. They rent out their retirement home until they are ready to retire. This is not a bad idea. It means you can use the rent money earned to pay the mortgage. So, in essence, someone else is paying off the mortgage on your retirement home. There are also tax benefits like interest payments on your mortgage that can be deducted and depreciation. You may find owning a rental is something very valuable in your current life, as well as preparing for retirement in the future.

Downsize Early

Generation Y or Millennials were born between 1980 and 1994. If you are a millennial, you may not be interested in downsizing yet but it would be good if you learned from the older generations what not to do before accumulating so much "stuff!"

This generation is currently between 26 years of age and 40 years of age. It is time to consider retirement if you are nearing age 40. Most people reach their peak income levels in their mid-40s and early 50s, so retirement should be on your mind. How much will you save for retirement and what those years look like, depend on what you do today.

This generation is divided into two groups, the Gen Y.1 and Gen Y.2. Some are still in early adulthood, starting new careers and getting married. Older millennials may already have bought a home and started a family. The contrast in the two groups is vast considering their priorities. However, the desire to own your own home is there, even for single adults. With this increased demand, the market prices become higher and this can affect the older generations.

The economy in the United States is very good at the present time. People that have delayed home-buying, are now seriously looking. It is a seller's market in most places.

Planning ahead is always a good thing.

Chapter 3

What Kind of Home Is Best For You?

Many opportunities exist today for the senior home buyer. It is a good time to be entering the "golden years." Age is no longer defined by numbers, but by activity. Many seniors are very active. If you can avoid health problems, you can live long and healthy up to 100 years or more.

Selling your larger home in your 60s, 70s, or 80s and buying a smaller, easier to maintain home is a wise choice. With people living longer, why shouldn't you have the most fun and stay active as long as possible? Spend the time you normally spend repairing and maintaining an older home, doing something you enjoy, like golfing or swimming or whatever you please. Leave the yard work to someone else or buy a place where the lawn is gravel or stone.

Your home is a very special place. If you've lived in it for 20 years, 30 years or even 40 years, you and your family have many memories there. It is hard to leave this special place, but you are not leaving the memories behind. They will go with you. Photographs are a great way to remember, and hopefully, you have many photos of the good times.

If you are a sentimental person and your emotions are making it hard to decide to downsize, think of your life like chapters in a book. You may have completed one chapter, and now it is time to turn the page to another chapter of your life.

Today, the chapters of our lives can be whatever we want to make them. Opportunities exist today, that our grandparents did not have. Retirement is not just waiting for the end to happen. It is more like making decisions to embrace change and do some things we have never been able to do before. When you are working 5 or 6 days a week, getting away for a week or even a weekend is very difficult. Now, you have the time and with downsizing there is less expense. So hopefully, you will have more cash to spend doing what you've always wanted to do.

I have a friend that recently returned from her first cruise. She had dreamed of taking a cruise for a long time but never had the time or resources. She is in the process of downsizing and has already experienced some good changes.

Fear of change paralyzes most people. Not all change is good, but neither is all change bad. Ask your friends what experiences they have had with downsizing, if fear is stopping you.

Have you heard about the 90-year-old lady that went skydiving? She confronted her fears and did what she had always wanted to do. She has another skydiving trip planned next year. What could you do differently if you downsized?

Knowing the area of the country where you want to move is important and knowing the lifestyle you want is something that you need to determine before you look for a new home. If your health is a concern and you need to move near relatives, that has answered these questions. But if you are healthy and just need to free up cash, your time, energy, there are many options and areas of the country to consider.

Some people are afraid to make a change because they feel they cannot afford it. In Chapter 6, you will learn about some mortgages that may help you make that change financially.

Open your mind to the possibilities. But first, let's decide on the lifestyle you are seeking.

What kind of home is best? Here are some options:

Single family home-A single family home is a home on a lot by itself. You have your own yard, separate driveway, and more privacy. You also have the yard to take care of unless you can afford to pay someone to do it for you.

Again, there are lots of communities, especially in the South, where gravel yards are common. No watering, no mowing, no fertilizing, is a nice thing. A gravel yard can be put in on any lot if the subdivision rules allow for it. It may cost several thousand dollars to do it but it is worth it in the long run. A plastic sheet is put down on the ground to keep weeds from growing through it and gravel is put on top several inches thick. It is landscaped with a few trees or plants, generally cacti because most gravel yards are in warm areas like Texas, Arizona and Florida where cactus and succulents thrive.

Single family homes are in most neighborhoods and have every age range living there. A smaller single family home with less upkeep may meet your needs.

Over age 55 subdivisions- There are, however, subdivisions that only allow people over the age of 55 to live there. This restriction can be a part of the deed to the property. When you have subdivisions like this, there is usually an HOA (Homeowner's Association). These associations have lots of power to make rules about what you can put outside your home, what color you can paint your home, how many cars you have in your driveway, etc. There is a monthly or yearly fee for the HOA. These fees are charged for the enforcement of rules and the maintenance of common property.

Common areas can contain clubhouses, swimming pools, parking areas, libraries, playgrounds and golf courses. Your fees can also include lawn services for your home. Living in a subdivision like this can have many advantages. All your neighbors will be of the same age and noise will be at a minimum usually. Common areas are nice to use and you do not have to maintain them yourself. Best of all, you and your neighbors share the expense.

Many times, these neighborhoods have fencing and a locked gate. The extra safety this affords can be peace of mind for older residents. Stopping at the gate and using a clicker or keypad to open it takes a little time, but it is a good safety feature.

If you like privacy and living in a **separate house or townhome** similar to a duplex, but want more amenities with a shared cost, consider an over age 55 single family community. There are communities like this in most every state.

In Texas, there are some in the San Antonio area and Georgetown areas that I am familiar with. The homes are newer and come in half a dozen sizes and designs. They can vary in price from mid-range to expensive. They often have clubhouses with libraries, gyms, cafes, swimming pools, tennis courts, daily activities and some even offer minor emergency services. There are so many nationwide, and they vary in size and price. You can find what you are looking for.

Florida is a retirement haven and has been for decades. The warm weather attracts "snow birds" in the winter, but many are moving to Florida full time as we see population growth reaching new levels.

One area I am familiar with is The Villages. It is one of the largest age restricted, active adult communities in the world. With 90 miles of golf cart paths, it is continuing to grow. It occupies parts of three counties in Florida. You can live in the Villages and never have to leave. All the little shops and big stores, restaurants and medical facilities are there for you.

Homes of various sizes and prices attract many seniors. Florida has lots to offer recreationally, too. Fishing, beaches, Disney World, Everglades, boating, and golfing are just some of the attractions. Living in Florida can be like being on vacation every day.

Manufactured Home Parks- One-third of all baby boomers have limited funds, you may be in this category. Or, you may want to save as much money as possible for your retirement. If so, how can you downsize and make life easier? There are manufactured home parks where you can buy a home for much less than a conventional stick built home. These parks are located everywhere but especially in Texas, Florida, Arizona and California where baby boomers like to retire. The warm weather is a draw for older people not wanting to deal with snow in the wintertime.

You can buy a manufactured home in one of these parks and pay a monthly fee for the lot rent. This fee is usually several hundred dollars a month and pays for your water bill and maintenance of common areas. You own your own home and can still homestead it, but only pay taxes on the home, not the lot. This makes senior living easier as well.

Most of these parks have amenities like the other communities. Clubhouses and swimming pools are the norm. Monthly fees maintain these facilities. Unlike HOAS where the residents have a vote, the owners of these parks make the rules.

The best thing about living in these parks is the low cost of housing, but many times you cannot move your home off the lot if you want to move it. Also, there are times when the owners want to upgrade their parks and make the residents move their older homes. There are limited places where older manufactured homes can be moved. If you don't have land in the country without restrictions, you may not find a place to move it. Check out the rules before you buy in a community like this. If you don't get along with the owner of the park, it could hurt you financially if you have to move because of bad relations.

Manufactured homes in Texas are governed by TDHCA, Texas Department of Housing and Community Affairs in Austin. You must have a permit to move a manufactured home in Texas, and TDHCA knows where every manufactured home is located in Texas. If you need owner information, this is where you get it. Manufactured homes have specific rules on transport, location, set-up, and titles. Check with them before you buy a manufactured home. I am sure other states have similar agencies and rules.

There is a difference between manufactured homes and modular homes. A manufactured home is built in a factory and moved to a location with a large truck. A modular home is built in pieces in a factory and assembled on the lot. The rules for these two kinds of homes are different. The building guidelines are also different, and this affects insurance rates too.

The adult parks I have been describing have only manufactured homes in them, not modular homes. A modular home is considered part of the land, the property, for taxing purposes. Manufactured homes have titles like a car or other vehicle. They are not part of your lot or property unless you surrender your title and tell the tax office you will never move the home. It can then become part of the property. There are many reasons why someone would do this.

Again, we were discussing parks where you do not own the land but only rent a lot by the month. Surrendering a title and making it part of the property only occurs in the country on land you own yourself.

I was in Florida recently, and I found a manufactured home park where the residents actually own their own lot. This is very rare in today's market. There was an HOA fee, but it was very inexpensive and it covered common areas. This particular park had lots of amenities which made living there quite fun. It was for people over age 55, but they allowed a certain number of residents to be younger. There are regulations regarding this and every park must comply. This is a good way to retire and lower your expenses if you are so inclined.

Condominiums and Apartments- Condominiums and apartments offer less maintenance for the older resident. However, your privacy is diminished living close to other people. Sometimes, noise can be a problem if you have adjoining walls, but most senior condo associations have rules about noise.

The difference between a condominium and an apartment is air space between two walls for the condominium and only one wall with no air space for the apartment. Living in a senior development has many advantages. Not only is noise regulated, but large pets are usually not allowed. There is no need to worry about toys left on the lawn or souped-up car engines in the retirement complex.

Owning your own condo or apartment gives you more freedom and is the choice of many seniors. I have relatives that love them and would not want to live anywhere else.

A big plus are the common areas and community meeting rooms. Most times, there are scheduled activities and this gives you a place to meet friends and just hang out. I know of one condo complex that has a big pot luck dinner once a week and card games, dominoes, dancing, shuffleboard, bingo, quilting, and even special guests and entertainment regularly scheduled. You may also reserve a meeting room with or without a kitchen for a private gathering making the need for a larger home null and void.

Some condo complexes have no common areas except walking trails. Without a common meeting room, getting to know neighbors is more difficult. Each person has their preference, and many people may prefer these kinds. Without the upkeep of community rooms, HOA fees may be less expensive.

Tiny Homes and Granny Pods

Tiny Homes are the new thing. One small town in West Texas has re-platted lots in town for tiny homes. New communities are springing up in other areas as well.

The lots have been re-drawn smaller and new ordinances were passed to allow for smaller square footage in these new homes. This town had suffered a population decrease for many years because of a lack of jobs. When they allowed tiny homes to be built, retirees on fixed incomes came and the town is now flourishing again.

A tiny home can come ready assembled with all the furnishings you need. With all the appliances, furniture, bedding, drapes, completely ready to move in. Or a tiny home can be a shell with the studs showing, where the buyer insulates, puts up the drywall, puts in the electrical and plumbing systems and finishes out the home. You can buy these tiny homes in various stages of finished work. The prices are very reasonable.

You must have a piece of ground to place them on. Check with the city clerk or county clerk to know what restrictions exist in your area before you buy a lot.

Preparing a foundation or site can be expensive. If you need to drill a well or put in a septic system, the savings may not be there. Put your math skills to work and consider all options before you decide which kind of home suits your needs the best. Also, consider the advantages of buying a new home versus a used home.

Grandma Pods in backyards are even becoming popular today. Not all subdivisions allow for these, but many do. If you want to live near family but still want independence, this may be the perfect solution for you. Retirees often sleep later and dislike the noise a busy family brings. That is a common irritant when several generations live in the same house. A Granny Pod in the backyard gives retirees privacy and gives the children peace of mind, knowing the older parents are nearby and easy to check on. Many full-time RVer's find having a Tiny House or a Granny Pod brings a sense of security for when they can no longer travel.

Before you need Assisted Living

As we age, simple tasks become harder. Many seniors do not have family members nearby that can drop over and perform those tasks that we once did with no problem. Fortunately, there are home service companies today that do little things that require standing on a ladder, or things that require more strength than we now have. Takl is one of those companies that will do anything from changing light bulbs to cleaning rain gutters, fixing your television, taking out trash, whatever you need.

If you need someone to come fix dinner, buy groceries, or just come by for a visit, Visiting Angels is a company that comes with good reviews. Staying in your home longer is made possible by companies that provide services like these.

A new trend I am hearing more and more about is one where several friends move in together, and share expenses and chores. This is working well, especially for women.

There are many options for seniors today that want to downsize and make their lives easier. Determining your lifestyle needs and planning ahead is key to a smooth transition when downsizing.

Chapter 4

What to Look For When Buying

Now that we have discussed the various kinds of homes available to you, you may have some idea of what kind of home will suit your needs best. There are many plusses and minuses with each one. After you consider each one, you will begin to know what the most important factors are to you. Is it privacy you want the most? Is it security? Is a fence around the entire property and a locked gate best for your needs? Do you want more of a community setting with close neighbors next door? The things most important to you and your desired lifestyle will dictate which type of home you should look for.

As you walk through homes being shown by your REALTOR®, you will see all the usual things, but let's look a little deeper. **Let's look with the *eyes of a home inspector*.** You may find problems that would eliminate the home from your list of potential buys before you waste time and money on professional home inspections.

Even if you are buying new construction as opposed to older homes that have been lived in, you need to look closely and hire an inspector. Many new homes today are not built as well as homes built previously. The lumber is not as good in many carpenters' minds, and other materials can vary in quality. The building methods involve speed with an eye for profit more than excellence. The lack of craftsmanship today is a testament of quantity versus quality.

You will find homes with floor plans you like and floor plans you don't like. Finding the right floor plan for your current and future needs is important, but in this chapter you will learn some important details to look for in each room of the new home before you contract to purchase the property. Looking for these little details along the way will save you time and money by eliminating certain houses from your list.

The location is most important. Do you want to be near your children or grandchildren? Your location may help to make your decision about the kind of home you need. Most home styles are available in all areas of the country, especially if you want to live near a larger city. For people wanting to live in more rural areas, the options are more limited.

After you have chosen your location, city, town, it is time to decide which type home you need to look at first. Your first impression may change after you see what is on the market in your desired location and desired price range.

What should you look for when you first go house hunting? You want a home with a good foundation, good roof, good structure, and you want to know all the flaws of the home before you purchase. The major systems in a home need to be in good condition or you will be making repairs in the near future.

Let's assume you are looking at a condo community with amenities like a clubhouse and pool. Now, imagine walking through the home with a REALTOR®. It is the first time you have been to the community. Look hard at the entrance. Is it fenced and gated? Is it easy to enter with the right code? Are there many cars coming and going? Is there easy access to the property from the road, or is it on a busy intersection?

Many people coming and going on a busy highway can be dangerous. One complex I used to sell condos in had an exit onto a busy road, and the cars had to make a left turn. It was a great complex, but getting onto the highway was dangerous. There were no traffic lights nearby, and the speed limit for oncoming traffic in the opposite direction was too fast for cars waiting to turn onto the highway. Numerous accidents occurred at this location. Access is important to consider.

Is there noise from the highway? Will this be acceptable in the future when the newness of your purchase wears off? Is there ample parking? Will you always have a place to park when you drive up in the rain? Is there a private garage or carport? Or do you have to share parking with others?

Now, imagine you have stopped and you are out of the car. Is there a sweet atmosphere about the place? Are there flower beds? Are they neatly kept? Is there grass to mow? Who maintains these things? What kind of maintenance expense is required by each home owner? These are important questions to ask.

The front door says a lot about a house. Is it nice and in good repair? Is it welcoming to visitors? What kind of impression do you already have of this house?

Yes, I am asking a lot of questions before you even enter the front door. Was the sidewalk in good condition, could you add a ramp to this property if needed, did you notice the roof as you drove up? Your REALTOR® should be looking at all these things for you as well. Do not rely on them, however, do your own research.

With every house, there is a **seller's disclosure**. This is a document you should look at as you are touring the home. It will tell you if there is anything wrong with the house, per the seller's acknowledgement. If you find things wrong with the house that are not listed on the seller's disclosure, bring this to the REALTOR'S® attention. These things need to be addressed in any contract you might write. Always have everything in writing!

The first room is the foyer or entryway. I always look around the door for signs of water penetration. I try the door and make sure it is properly attached and does not hang when opening and closing. I want the door area to be well lighted inside and out. Of course, you want a deadbolt and keyed entry. Remember, to re-key your new home after you move in. Locked doors are the biggest deterrent to crime.

As you walk into the living room, what is the first thing that catches your eye? This is the focal point of the room. Everyone has likes and dislikes but in this book, we want to discuss the practical side of buying a new home. Is the floor covering in good condition? Are the floors level; if not this could be a sign of foundation issues. Are the walls painted a pleasing color, and is the paint in good condition? Painting can be a big expense.

Is there a fireplace in the living room? It needs to be checked for sure. Is it dirty inside? Does it have soot buildup? You may want to have it professionally cleaned by the seller before you buy. It could also need some repair that you cannot see until after it is cleaned. This is just something to look out for if you are interested in the property.

Do the drapes, blinds and curtains stay with the sale? If not, this also can be a big expense.

Is there a dining room? Is it adjoining the living area? If there is no dining room, where will you have your meals? Is there an eat-in kitchen with room for a table and chairs? Is there a breakfast bar or nook?

Now, the next room should be the kitchen. There are many things to look for in the kitchen. Look at not only the size of the room, the amount of cabinets, the countertop space, but the appliances. Is there a refrigerator, range, microwave, dishwasher, disposal, and trash compactor? Are there other appliances also? What is the age of the appliances? This is a big expense when they wear out, and most times, they wear out at the same time. Often, you can buy a home warranty policy with the purchase of the home that will take care of things like this when they stop working. Sometimes, the seller will offer to pay for the home warranty. Be sure to ask for this in your purchase contract.

Is the kitchen too large, or is it too small? For me, this is an important question. I have had both. Too large and you have to walk too much. This could be a problem later if you have trouble walking. If it is too small, it is not easy to prepare meals. Once I had a kitchen that was too small. I hated it! I could never find the right pan because it was stacked tightly with other pans and other things in front of it. I would have to move many things just to find what I was looking for. Many times, I had to get on my knees to do this. It hurt. So find the right size kitchen for you. It will make a big difference in the enjoyment of your new home.

Is there room to navigate a wheelchair? Can you make this home ADA compliant if needed?

Next thing in the kitchen to look at is the sink. The sink could have problems. Is it in good condition? Do the faucet handles turn on and off properly? Is there leaking anywhere?

Look under the sink. Is it leaking or is there evidence of leaking in the past that was not repaired? You can see if the floor of the cabinet is warped. Move the cleaners if you must, but look. Plumbing is expensive to fix, and so are wooden cabinets if they have had water penetration.

Look in the corners of the ceilings in every room for water damage. Your inspector will look for all these things, but a preliminary viewing by you can eliminate many of the homes being shown.

Floors and windows need to be inspected in every room. Every window should open and lock. Turn each light on and off to make sure they work properly. Light switches are easily fixed but electrical problems are not.

These are just some of the things you need to check as you are walking through a home if you have any interest in buying. As you go into the bedrooms, check all the areas we have talked about. In the bedrooms, I like to consider the lighting. Will I be able to sleep comfortably in this room? Will the sun come into the window in the morning? Is there noise near the window or outside wall of this room? These are just some things to consider.

How many bedrooms do you need? Will one bedroom be enough? Do you need room for company? Do you need an extra room for an office or hobby room? If you do not need the extra space, choose to do without. After all, you are downsizing. You are lowering your expenses and making life easier for yourself.

Just like my kitchen being too small, choose a home with the right size for your needs. Don't overdo but don't underdo either. If you have things you cannot part with, find a place where you can keep your treasures that are most important to you. You want life to be happy and easy, so finding the right size place is vital to your happiness.

I am a baby boomer myself. As I write these words, I am preparing what I will keep and what I will let go in my next move. I have a wonderful old china cabinet that belonged to my aunt. I have loved it and cherished it for many years. It will go to my son or grandchildren, and so will many of the things it holds today. I have vases, plates, figurines, and certain articles that belonged to my grandparents in the cabinet.

I want to give these things away while I am still here. I want to see their faces when they receive these things I have held dear for so many years. They will get them when I am gone, anyway. Why shouldn't I give them away now? It will free up some space in my new home when I am ready to downsize. It makes sense to do it now.

Now, let's walk into the bathroom. Bathrooms are one of the most important rooms in your house. We never know when we might need a wheelchair. So, choose a new home with enough room in the bathroom. Are the counters the right height for you? Is the tub or shower what you want? If not, could it be changed and if so, how much would that cost? It might be too much or it might not, so check with a contractor if you are interested in a particular home that needs some modification. Your Realtor® can give you some names of contractors in your area.

Again, check the plumbing in the bathroom. Check the floors, windows, walls and ceilings like the other rooms. Now, is the door at least 32 inches wide? A wheelchair is 28 inches wide. A door that is 36 inches wide is much better. You must have room for your hands on the wheels.

Can you get in the shower or tub easily? Are there grab bars installed? Is the floor made of a material that is slippery? All these are things to be mindful of.

When downsizing, look at wasted spaces in your new home to add some extra storage. A taller vanity in the bathroom might add some much needed space if you are not concerned with it being wheelchair accessible. Shelving can be added under tall vanities and cabinets. Shelving can also be added to walls and small cabinets can be placed in wasted space areas. Book shelves can display an assortment of things, not just hold books.

When living in a smaller space, storage can be a big problem. Today's multipurpose furniture has options, such as ottomans and benches that open up to provide storage for blankets or large items. Under the bed storage can make a room more functional. The newest closet arrangers make a small space much more useful. Good organization can also make a smaller home feel bigger. You need a place for everything you intend to keep, but after you downsize your things, that space will be much smaller.

Lastly, let's look at the utility room. Does the washer and dryer stay with the property? Are they in good condition? Is there a utility sink? Check the plumbing here as well. Are the connections done properly and is the dryer venting to the outside? Many times, the dryer is vented into the attic. That is a code violation in most areas now. It will need to be changed before your loan is approved. The party, whether buyer or seller, that pays for these changes needs to be listed in any contract, and this is a negotiable repair.

The backdoor goes into the backyard or side yard. This door should be a solid core door. If it does not have a window, it should have a peep hole like the front door. What kind of locks are on the doors? Are they good quality? Each needs a deadbolt and locking doorknob. Look for signs of burglarized entry. Hopefully, you will not find this, but it is something to keep in mind. Look carefully at the door frame for scratches or nicks in the wood, and if it has recently been painted.

Inspections and Agent Representation

The most expensive parts of a home to repair are the foundation, the roof, the heating and air conditioning system, the plumbing system, the electrical system, and if in the country, the well and septic systems, of course. These are the things you want to inspect carefully. If you make an offer on a home, you will also want to get a home inspection. The inspections can be numerous depending on what the home has to offer and where it is located.

My last home had a home inspection by a licensed home inspector. I also had a water report by the county and also by the state since I had a well. My septic system was inspected. My roof was inspected and all these inspections were by different people at my expense.

Sure, inspections cost a lot of money, but it is important to know what you are buying. If you find problems during the inspections, many of these things can be repaired at the seller's expense. These are negotiable items. Your REALTOR® will help you negotiate these things if they are representing you as a buyer.

I provide a list of local inspectors and ask my clients to choose which ones they use. I never recommend any inspectors. I do highly suggest they personally check references for the inspectors. I never take referral fees from service providers, but some real estate agents do. Ask your agent if they get a fee for referrals to service agents. I think this could be a conflict of interest, therefore; I do not think it is a wise thing to do.

Licensed and bonded home inspectors are licensed by the state and they must attend continuing education classes. Most inspectors come from a similar background professionally. I have known inspectors that worked as inspectors for the city or county before they were licensed as home inspectors. I have known general contractors and builders that became home inspectors. These inspectors generally are very knowledgeable about home construction and common building practices, including building codes for the area.

On the other hand, I have known people who became home inspectors because the money and hours appealed to them. Several well-known inspectors, I have known in the past, were never involved in the home industry at all. They took a few classes, passed a test, and became licensed. These inspectors rarely did a good job of inspecting a home for a potential buyer. A few times, they scared my buyers by telling them something entirely inaccurate about the home they wished to buy.

Agents have no recourse with a situation like this. The buyer is paying for the inspection and expects to get a good understanding of the problems or potential problems that come with a house. Every house will have a few things wrong that need to be repaired. No house is perfect. Sometimes, the inspector makes a big issue out of nothing. One inspector I used gave totally wrong information to my clients. When confronted with his mistakes, he denied them. Fortunately, my buyers hired another inspector to re-inspect the house and decided to buy. It was a good decision on their part.

A good inspector will provide a detailed report with full color pictures explaining every system and part of your new home. All areas will be inspected and pictures and descriptions will be provided on any repair that needs to be addressed. The inspector will check every electrical outlet and every appliance. They will climb onto the roof and go underneath the crawl space. The drains and plumbing will be checked. The lighting fixtures checked, the walls, the floors, the doors and windows also will be checked for full operation as intended when the home was built. The report will also discuss the condition of each item and the economic life remaining, giving the buyer an idea of when the item will need to be replaced. Home maintenance is an ongoing expense. Knowing future expenses ahead of time helps to ensure a fully informed and happy buyer transaction.

Most real estate agents do not have experience or knowledge concerning home construction. Do not rely on their opinions about the condition of a home. Some do however, like me, have lots of experience. I have built a few homes and buildings in the past. I have remodeled around 100 homes and some of those were total re-dos. With the knowledge I have, I will still always get an inspection. More than one opinion is best.

Is it important to have a buyer's agent in today's market?
Yes, it is! I cannot express how important it is to have someone to represent you and your interests. If you have not discussed this with your REALTOR® or agent at length and

signed a document listing the responsibilities of each party, you might not have representation. Make sure you do before you buy or sign a contract.

Some people do not care if they have representation or not. They feel they are well informed and able to make the decision without an agent or REALTOR'S® help. I have been in the business for forty years. I have seen many changes in the law, in attitudes, in the way of doing business. In Texas, we have strong laws regarding agent representation. Most REALTORS® and agents follow these laws, but some do not. It is up to you to be careful and aware when working with someone who is not knowledgeable about the laws and guidelines for agent representation. Each state is different. As a real estate broker, I would never buy a property without representation even for myself. It is too important. Things happen.

Note: In chapter 10, I discuss the difference between agents and Realtors®.

Confidentiality is one of the things you get with a fiduciary relationship. A fiduciary relationship is one where you have hired an agent to represent you. If the agent is representing the seller, they cannot represent you also. They could facilitate the transaction, but their loyalty is to the person they have a signed contract with.

So, in some states, it is common practice for buyers to use the seller's agent to write the contract. The buyer should be aware they may not have representation in this case scenario. The agent represents the seller. They have contracted to get the best possible price for the seller. The buyer has nobody to negotiate on their behalf. In Texas, I will only represent one party, the buyer or the seller at any given time.

Some states still have dual agency. In Texas, dual agency has become illegal. How can someone truly represent both sides?

If you do not have representation, your words can be told to the seller. "I like this house, but this is not the location I wanted. I would only be willing to give this amount for this property." Did you expect this conversation to be confidential?

If you want confidentiality, get a buyer's agent to represent you. It pays off in the long run, even if you have to pay out of your pocket for the services of a professional buyer's agent.

Any agent can act as a buyer's agent, but one that practices buyer agency regularly will do a better job. States are different and have different laws. Talk to your potential agent before you look at property. Get everything in writing!

The buyer agency contract may be more important for your bottom line than the contract to purchase your new home.

Some other things that a fiduciary relationship provides are **loyalty, obedience, disclosure, and accountability**. Is your real estate agent providing these things to you? If not, you may not be in a fiduciary relationship. At this stage of the game, isn't it best to have someone representing you in the purchase of maybe your last home? I personally want someone I can discuss things with and know my conversation will not be shared with anyone else. I want to put my trust in the professional that is helping me make the best decision concerning my new home and maybe my last residence.

Buying a smaller home and downsizing is a good thing. It will be easier to care for, have less taxes maybe, be closer to shopping and other destinations frequented, and give you more time and money to enjoy life.

Buyer Agents and Home Inspectors

help make your move less stressful.

Chapter 5

Taxes and Insurance

Everyone knows every house comes with a yearly bill for taxes and insurance. It is something we all dread. It comes around every year, no matter what!

If you have a mortgage on your home, chances are good that you also have an escrow account. Money is deposited every month into the account to pay for the taxes and insurance at the end of the year or when they come due. This money is part of your monthly house payment. You don't notice it as much when a little is taken each month from the house payment, rather than receiving a huge bill at the end of the year, like people without a mortgage payment receive.

That yearly bill can be a hard pill to swallow, especially if you have not budgeted for it. Owning your own home is a joy, but paying taxes is not much fun. And of course, insurance is a must even if your home is paid for and mortgage free. You must protect your investment.

Because we cannot get away from paying taxes and we must keep our homes insured, let's look at a few things about taxes and insurance.

Property taxes are paid on the assessed value of your property. What is assessed value? It is a number the tax assessor-collector uses when figuring your taxes. It is not market value. Market value is what your home would bring if you were selling it. Assessed value is very different and sometimes is less than half of market value. Different states have different rules in how they determine assessed value. You could call your local tax office and ask them how they determine assessed value.

Bottom line is this:

Assessed value multiplied by (X) Tax rate = Tax dollars ($) due at end of year

Therefore, you want your assessed value as small as possible if you are trying to save money in your retirement. You may want to do some research in your local tax offices if you are downsizing and selling your home and then possibly buying another home.

I made a move once, where I moved from an area with high assessed values to an area with lower assessed values. They determined these values completely differently. The latter place had lower taxes for a property valued at nearly the same market value. I was thrilled about this.

If you are over 65, there should be some extra deductions on your tax bill. You must visit the tax office and sign a document to get the deduction. You will get a homestead deduction also if this is your primary residence. Be sure and ask about every deduction that you might qualify for. Every state and even county is different.

Some places offer veteran deductions and also disability deductions. Just as the tax rates are different, so are the deductions that each area offers. Be sure to ask and sign up for all that apply to you. It will make retirement easier.

In most areas, if you are over 65, the county can* Freeze *your taxes. This means they can never raise the taxes you pay as long as you own your home and it is your primary residence.

If the assessed value goes up, your tax bill will not go up unless you make some major improvements after your taxes are frozen. Many times, taxes remain the same for a long period when they are frozen. You have to ask for this to be done. The tax office does not tell you about it. You have to ask! Every county is different, so check.

Frozen taxes can be transferred to another home in the same county in California. In Texas, you can transfer to a different county. Every state and county is different, but most places have some kind of provision for seniors. Widows and widowers can also apply for the freeze if they are 55 or older, and the taxes were previously frozen.

When you are thinking about downsizing, moving into a smaller home, easier to maintain and with less expense; remember Taxes and Insurances are a big consideration!

The area you choose to buy in can also determine the amount of taxes you will pay. Are you moving closer to relatives? If this is the case, you may not have as many options. If you have a lot of options though, take time to consider the areas' amenities and which ones are important to you. You will pay in a roundabout way for many of those options in the form of property taxes. Consider all these things.

My friend lives near a major league ballpark and her property taxes show it. She likes to go to the park occasionally but if she were retiring, which she is not at the present time, she might want to consider her location because of the high property taxes she pays. Ballparks, airports, buildings, universities, freeways all add to property taxes. If you need not be really close to these things, why pay for them. Live a little further away and your taxes can be less.

There are two things in life that are certain they say, "Death and Taxes."

I would like to add **"Insurance."**

Insurance, insurance, how I hate that word! It is a necessary evil, however. We must protect our home from all kinds of disasters.

Homeowner's insurance will protect your home if it burns down or is destroyed by various disasters. Homeowner insurance policies also cover your contents up to about forty percent of the value of your policy. This would include furniture, household goods, clothing, personal effects, even jewelry, guns, tools, whatever you have in your home.

Homeowner insurance policies cover partial losses as well. These can include hail, wind, rain, and other losses. Some vandalism is covered in some policies. Just like taxes being different in different parts of the country, insurance policies vary even more.

It is always good to work with a local agent that you can sit down with face to face and discuss what you are buying. You want to understand your coverage before you have a loss, not afterwards.

There is an insurance policy for everything you can imagine!

Flood insurance is something not everyone needs, but most agents will say more people need it than not. Even if you do not live near a body of water or a river or creek, you may eventually be flooded. Every county has a flood plain map and they are always changing. Realtors® keep up with the changes because the flood plain map determines what kind of insurance a buyer needs when buying a home. If you are getting a mortgage, the mortgage company requires you to buy flood insurance if you are located within certain flood zones.

Your homeowner's insurance will not pay for rising water like from a river or creek. Too much rain, too quickly can flood drainage ditches, and culverts may not handle it and it rises onto your property. ***Only flood insurance pays for that.***

Note: I want to add that water seeping up from the ground, such as in a basement, requires flood insurance. Homeowner's insurance does not pay for water damage from this as well.

Make sure you check the Current flood plain maps before you buy your new home. Recently, several states have been inundated with heavy rain and flooding like never before. Farms are underwater and cannot plant their fields this year at all. Many of these people, when interviewed, said they had never seen this amount of rain or flooding in their area. Many have lived there for generations. Flooding occurs in areas not known for flooding. Having flood insurance is wonderful when you need it. Only you can make the decision whether it is worth taking the risk or not.

Retiring and downsizing? Saving money? Should you move where you need flood insurance? All these are questions only you can answer. If you move to a coastal community, or on water, flood insurance is a necessity.

Windstorm Insurance is another insurance you must have if you live on the coast. Hurricanes don't happen often, but when they do, the destruction is immense. Tornadoes can come with a hurricane or just in a thunderstorm, and the windstorm insurance will cover what is not covered in homeowner's insurance. It is mandatory if you live on the coast in Texas. I'm sure it must be the same for Florida and California as well. Sunny locations with beautiful water often come with big insurance bills. This is something a retiree should also consider.

Sinkhole Insurance is something you might need in Florida. Every area of the country has its own natural disasters, and this is one for Florida.

I am sure there is insurance for volcanoes and for earthquakes too. Like I said earlier, there is insurance for everything. The person downsizing wants to take all these things into consideration when deciding where to move if saving money is a consideration. There are pros and cons with every area. Sunny locations can mean more outside activities and less heating bills. However, there are air conditioning bills to look at as well. Weigh all before you decide. This can be the best move of your life!

Chapter 6

Reverse Mortgages and Other Loans

A Fictional Example:

Dorothy sat by the window watching the snow fall. It was a cold afternoon, and the weather had turned bad in the past few days. No sunshine was forecast for the coming week, and her mood was as gloomy as the skies.

The coffee in her favorite mug tasted cold and stale. Her hair appeared grayer today than yesterday. When George passed, her hope left like he did. What good times they had together, but now the future was bleak. Even a smile from the neighbor's child building a snowman outside her window, would not lift the corners of her mouth.

Grief and depression were not things she handled well. As the days passed, another reality struck. How would she pay the bills?

There were high utility bills with the cold weather. Food, clothing, medical, auto payments, gasoline, insurance; that dastardly bill that never quits rising. Stress and worry were her new norms. The biggest monthly bill, however, dwarfed all the others put together. The house payment!

She could cut back on some things. The heat could be turned down low. She could do without lots of extras and even cut the food bill, but the house payment was a must that had to be paid on time. Her home could be in jeopardy. She shuddered to think what would happen to her if she lost it. Where would she go? What would she do? She never wanted to be a burden to her grown children.

Then, there were the memories of all the good times in this lovely place. The curtains she sewed for the windows, the mural she painted in the kitchen, the garden she and her husband planted together every year, even the grandchildren's footprints cemented in the patio, added to those great memories. It could all be gone in a matter of months. How could she keep up the payments on this beautiful home, her home? She loved it here and never wanted to leave.

The despair was in her eyes, even her posture showed the effects of the worry in her mind. Who could she turn to? "Does anybody have an answer to my problem," she would cry to herself.

There were many commercials on television expounding the virtues of **reverse mortgages**. It made little sense to her. She did not understand the very concept. She thought it was probably a scam. Who could explain these reverse mortgages and was it even an option for her?

She called her Realtor®. Maybe selling the house was the only solution. A very nice lady came to visit and gave her an estimate of the value of her home. Selling was not what she wanted to do, but it seemed like the only answer.

Fortunately, Dorothy called the right Realtor®. One that had Dorothy's best interests in mind, and this Realtor® was very knowledgeable about reverse mortgages. She gave Dorothy options! Dorothy could sell and move into a smaller house with smaller payments, or she could apply for a reverse mortgage.

Dorothy learned a reverse mortgage is like any other mortgage, a loan based on the current value of the home. The loan proceeds are used to pay off the existing mortgage, and the remainder of the money is given to the borrower. She could pay off her current mortgage and have no monthly payment. If there was extra money left over after her current mortgage was paid, the remainder would go to Dorothy. She could use the money to pay off other bills or use it for a supplement to her income, or for whatever she wanted.

She could live in her home until she died or decided to move. That's when the new reverse mortgage would come due in one payment. This would comprise the amount she borrowed, plus any interest accrued from the time she received the reverse mortgage until she moved.

Dorothy had a lot of equity in her home because she and her husband had owned it for twenty years, and as they made the payments, the equity increased. Taking a reverse mortgage seemed like a good idea. Her children would inherit her home on her death but would be required to pay off the reverse mortgage loan if they wanted to keep the house. They were doing well and did not need the house or the money, so Dorothy applied for the reverse mortgage. She received the reverse mortgage and lived without a monthly mortgage payment for the rest of her life.

Dorothy had enough equity in her home to pay off the current mortgage and have some money left over. She could have used this money for anything she wanted. Instead, she invested the extra money she had and that passed to her children when she died. With interest and dividends earned over time, it increased to almost enough to pay off the new reverse mortgage loan. Her son added the extra money needed, and they retained Dorothy's home. They had memories there, as well. Dorothy's granddaughter moved in and the home stayed in this family from then on.

*****

Reverse mortgages are not for everyone but in this case, it worked well. Do you know of someone who could use a reverse mortgage to relieve stress and make their life better?

Many reverse mortgage companies offer good deals, but there are others that are not reputable. Be sure to check each one out thoroughly. Losing your home in your golden years would be a nightmare.

Talk to several mortgage loan originators, your financial planner, your attorney, or CPA if you are considering using a reverse mortgage. Learn everything you can about these types of loans before you decide.

Saving your home, your precious memories and giving yourself peace of mind is invaluable. A Reverse Mortgage may be your answer, but learn all you can before you decide.

Today, there are new programs with reverse mortgages

to actually **PURCHASE** a new home.

Talk to a loan originator

to find out more.

Now, let's look at other loans…

CONVENTIONAL LOANS

Most people use conventional loans instead of government insured loans. Conventional loans are usually easier to get and require a little less paperwork. Conventional loans require a higher credit score, however, so if your credit score is not that high, an FHA or VA loan might work better for you.

Do you know what your credit score is? Many seniors do not because many seniors have paid cash for things for many years and have bought nothing on credit for a while. It is easy to find out what your credit score is. There are many websites that allow you to do this, but Experian.com is a good one that does not charge you for the service. All U.S. residents may obtain a credit report free of charge once a year from all three major reporting companies: Experian, Equifax, and Trans Union through AnnualCreditReport.com. Other websites charge nominal fees for access on a monthly basis if you prefer to see it more often.

Knowing your credit score ahead of time can give you an opportunity to boost it a little if you need a better score. The higher your credit score is, the lower your interest rate will be, which means a smaller house payment.

Conventional loans can be obtained from mortgage companies or banks. The down payments can be as small as five percent (5%) or as much as twenty percent (20%). Usually, if you put more money down, you will get a smaller interest rate as well. A good rule of thumb is one percentage

(1%) rate difference in interest makes about a hundred dollars ($100.00) difference in your monthly payment on a median priced home. That is a lot!

Today, there are financial calculators all over the Internet. I had one on my website when I was actively selling real estate. Many Realtors® have calculators on their websites and so do mortgage companies. Use one of these to estimate your monthly payment and you will know what price homes to look for. These calculators save lots of time.

A conventional loan will take from thirty days to a full two months or more to process. There are many steps in getting a home loan. You must provide documentation of income, expenses, savings, stocks, bonds, all assets and all obligations. Bank records going back at least three months will be required. Your funds for the down payment will need documentation too. Your loan officer will explain all this to you. If you currently own a home, your plans for your current house will be reviewed, whether you plan on selling it now or leasing it out. You must show you have the funds to pay for the mortgage during the process of selling. If you are planning on leasing your current home, the projected income is not counted now, as you are still living in it. After you lease it out, there is a certain period of time that is required before the money can be counted as stable income.

It is wise to gather all your documentation before you make application for your loan. There will always be things asked for that you did not anticipate, but doing as much as you can ahead of time saves headaches. Having a good loan officer can make the difference in the whole process being smooth and easy or hard and even difficult.

I have used many, many loan officers in the past. I have helped my clients find the loan they needed that worked best for them and then helped them find someone they felt comfortable with. A good loan officer will be available most of the time. It is a hard job, but a good loan officer must be there when you need them. One of my best friends in the business is **Tony Stevenson**. He works in the Texas Hill Country and the San Antonio area.

I remember calling him on weekends and even on Sunday nights needing information or needing him to pre-qualify a client. He has always been there for me, and he is always pleasant to work with. He has a great attitude and has been very helpful to my clients. There are times when a client cannot get pre-qualified for many reasons, but Tony has been optimistic and helped some of my clients increase credit scores or do different things that helped them qualify later. He is a man that follows up on clients and continues to work for them even when it is a difficult transaction. This is the kind of loan officer that works for you, and not just for a paycheck. He is the kind you want.

I asked Tony to share some insights with me and he said, *"There are three basic things for qualifying for a home loan. They are as follows:*

You must have good credit

You must be able to afford to make the payment.

You must have enough funds $$ to close.

Sounds easy enough-right? Of course, there are more details to each of these. That is why it so important to find a "Local" Mortgage Lender. Find a local loan officer who will explain the process from application to closing; a Loan Officer who knows the area and local REALTORS®. Find a lender that offers in-House Processing, Closing, Funding, and Underwriting. When you use "local" folks you will find the mortgage process a lot easier and faster, in my opinion.

With "Internet Lending" you are really just another faceless number. Your local Loan Officer will take pride in offering you their best service. They know they may see you in the local grocery store or watching sports with their kids. Your local Loan Officer will be able to show you the differences between certain loan programs too. If someone has credit challenges, the Loan Officer will help guide them so they may soon be able to qualify for a Mortgage. Finally, remember this, "cheaper doesn't always translate into better."

So what is the key word here? "Local". Find a local Loan Officer and REALTOR® and you will be closer than you think to obtaining the American dream of home ownership!"

Thank you, Tony Stevenson, for giving us these suggestions. Your input is very helpful.

Tony has been in the business for a long time and if you need help in the Texas Hill Country or San Antonio area, please email him at stevenson1961@gmail.com. He can provide you with up to date information on loans and interest rates.

Government Insured Loans

What is a government insured loan? A government insured loan is one where the government assures the repayment of the loan to an approved lender through mortgage insurance.

In foreclosure situations, it lessens the risk for the lender. These loans are commonly known as FHA or VA loans. VA loans are for veterans and their families only, but FHA is for everyone.

These loans have good interest rates and often have smaller closing costs for the borrower. Sometimes, the seller has to pay more closing costs with these loans than with a conventional loan. Most, younger people use these loans because down payments and closing costs are less and that enables them to buy a home sooner. It may cost the seller more, but most sellers agree to accept contracts with these kinds of loans because it increases the number of people that can buy their home.

Seniors should not discount using FHA or VA loans even if they have the extra cash needed for larger down payments and closing costs. Oftentimes, it is better and more cost effective to go this way. It does take longer and there is more paperwork involved. If you have the time and patience, it can pay big dividends. There is an extra inspection done with one of these loans that conventional loans do not require. That means that a few more repairs may need to be done before the loan can close. This is a deterrent for the seller, but a benefit for the buyer.

Your loan officer can explain all the differences to you and show you which one is best for your situation. *Get pre-approved before you look for homes.* It makes sense, and a pre-approved buyer may get a better deal on a house.

Conventional loans do not have the assurance that the government will pay back the loan if the borrower defaults, therefore, the interest rates can be higher. The mortgage company is taking the risk.

Any time the down payment is less than twenty percent (20%), there is also the cost for an insurance policy to cover the difference. This is called MIP, Mortgage Insurance Premium for FHA loans, or PMI, Private Mortgage Insurance for conventional loans.

For example, in a conventional loan, let's say you are paying a five percent (5%) down payment. That means you are fifteen percent (15%) short of the down payment needed to qualify without a PMI payment. The monthly payment for your loan will include Principal, Interest, Taxes, and Insurance (often called PITI) plus the PMI monthly amount. If you had paid twenty percent down (20%) you could have avoided the PMI payment and your monthly mortgage payment would have been less.

Example: **Conventional Loan** $ 200,000 purchase price

5% down payment	$ 10,000
95% loan amount	190,000

Interest rate   4% example

Amortized for 30 years fixed rate

Principal and Interest	$ 907.09
Insurance (1.5%)	250.00
Taxes (2.0%)	333.33
PMI	125.08
Total Monthly Payment	$1,616.00

Now let's look at what it will cost to close on a loan using the previous example.

On the same Conventional Loan:

Down Payment	$ 10,000.00
Prepaids	5,145.66

Fixed	4,764.63
Total Amount to Close	$ 19,910.29

Now, you are asking what are prepaids and fixed expenses. Prepaids are your insurance, one full year plus several months that is put into an escrow account so the mortgage company can pay it when it comes due next year at this time. Prepaids also include your taxes that will be due now, if any, plus several months to go into escrow as well. Again, so the mortgage company can pay them when they become due. Having an escrow account ensures that taxes and insurance are always paid up to date. It is a convenience for the new homeowner. PMI is also included in the prepaids.

The Fixed expenses will include attorney fees, escrow fees, appraisal, inspections, courier fees, mortgagee title policy, prepaid interest until the first day of the month and anything else that is charged to the buyer. Your loan officer will estimate all of these things in your first meeting. They will be updated periodically as the loan progresses, and you will have a final statement ready just before closing. This will tell you the amount to bring to closing in the form of a cashier's check or money order. The money can also be wired into the title company's account before closing.

Let's compare a conventional loan to an FHA loan. We will use the same figures we used in the previous example and see what kind of differences there are.

Example: **FHA Loan** $ 200,000 purchase price

3.5% down payment	7,000
96.5% loan amount	193,000
4% interest rate	
Principal and interest	$ 936.40
Insurance	250.00
Taxes	333.33
MIP	136.71
Total Monthly Payment	$ 1,656.00

As you compare the conventional loan with the FHA loan, you can see a larger down payment on the conventional loan makes a lot of difference. Putting down more money on the down payment (a difference of $3,000.00), the monthly payment is $40.00 a month less.

Now, let's compare the closing costs of the conventional loan to the FHA loan.

On the FHA Loan:

Down Payment	$ 7,000.00
Prepaids	5,475.06
Fixed	4,360.46
Total Amount to Close	$ 16,835.52

If you have bought homes before, you already know most of this information. However, some people have never bought a home before, and the process of obtaining financing is scary. A good loan officer can relieve the stress and guide you gently through the whole transaction.

VA Loans

If you are fortunate enough to be a veteran and can obtain a VA loan, your monthly payment on the previous example could be $1,559.00 with a zero down payment. You would need to bring $7,008.00 to closing. Do you see why I say going VA is a good option if you are a veteran?

Your out of pocket expense will vary depending on the area in which you are buying. For this example, I used 2% for taxes and 1.5% for insurance. If these percentages change because of your area, your closing costs will also change. These examples are for educational purposes only. A recent VA home purchase in my area had closing costs at only $1700.00, so the amount of taxes and insurance you will be paying makes a big difference.

IF you are a disabled veteran and receiving compensation for medical issues related to your military service, the VA Funding Fee may be waived. The VA Funding Fee is similar to the PMI or MIP on other loans. This is a good reason to use a VA loan if you are a disabled veteran. The VA has the final word on whether you qualify for the VA funding fee to be waived. Seniors often think of VA loans for younger people, but in this case, it can help the older generation substantially.

If this could be waived in a VA loan because you are disabled from medical issues related to your service, you can save a lot of money. The VA funding fee is paid at one time at closing, or it can be added to the loan amount financed. It is best to work with a good loan officer that can share the advantages of the different loans and help you choose which one will work best for you. **Remember, you will need your DD214 if you are a veteran and choose a VA loan**.

All these figures are hypothetical and can vary to some degree. Every transaction is different and mortgage companies' fees also vary from company to company. It is good to compare mortgage companies just like you compare other types of businesses.

There is another kind of government loan called a **USDA loan**. It is available for people who live in rural areas of approximately 25,000 people or less. There are many guidelines with this kind of loan and you must qualify for all these. There is a zero down payment available with this loan, and if you live in a rural area, you might want to check it out. There is only a certain amount of money allocated by the government every year for these loans. If you are buying at the beginning of the year, there may be money available, but later in the year they often run out of funds. In that case, you would have to wait until the next year's funding or go with a different kind of loan.

Cash is another option.

Some people have cash saved for a new home or they have sold their current home and cash funds are available for the purchase of a new home. If this is your situation, you will be looking at two to four weeks to close on your new home. Funds will be verified and a title policy prepared, and this takes a little time after the contract is accepted and all the requirements met.

Real Estate as an Investment

Real estate has historically been a good, fairly stable investment. A home you can live in and enjoy, but also know that your money is in a fairly safe investment. When the stock market craters or other investments come with big risks, your home values stay pretty consistent. The market will always fluctuate and I have seen several recessions in my real estate career. When and IF the real estate market ever went down, when it recovered, it came back with a vengeance. When I calculated the appreciation numbers, the results were always excellent. So, in my opinion, investing in real estate is a good thing.

Chapter 7

Buying vs. Renting

Buying is more often preferred than renting, but there are good things about both and I wanted to share some thoughts about both options for downsizing.

Your financial situation and your health could be the determining factors in whether you choose to buy or rent.

If you choose to buy, you will be putting down some money for a down payment or paying cash. We looked at mortgages in the preceding chapter. Your thoughts may change after you read this book and reconsider what is best for your situation.

Having a home that is paid off, free and clear of a mortgage brings peace of mind. However, not everyone is in that position today. There are many options available to make life easier and are discussed in this book.

What are the advantages to owning your home versus renting a home? Stability is number one. You may stay in your home as long as you desire when you own your home. If you have a mortgage, it must be paid and of course, taxes and insurance must also be paid. This will insure your home stays in your possession. Many people, like me, love the fact they own their home. It is a good feeling and nothing like "going home" when you've been away.

If you have a mortgage, you can deduct the cost of the interest payments on your income tax return. You can also deduct several other things and when you sell, you will not pay income tax on any profit up to a certain point. This is a good way to increase your net worth.

Equity build-up and appreciation can be quite substantial. So, just because you are of retirement age does not mean you stop making money.

If you own your home, the freedom of changing your home anyway you please is yours. Want to paint a wall purple? You can! Want to re-landscape your yard? You can! Want to build a patio with a fire pit? You can! Those choices are all yours, with the exception of HOA rules if you live in such a community. If you are renting, these are not options. You have what you have, and any changes are made by your landlord only.

I believe homeownership, which is a right and freedom, is a wonderful thing. Anyone who can, should own!

I bought my first home when I was only sixteen years old. I have been a Realtor® and broker for forty years. I have bought and sold more than a hundred homes for myself personally. I have sold thousands of homes to clients. I love helping people buy a home that can bring stability to their lives, increase their wealth and help them have special memories with their families.

I believe homeownership is something very special. If possible to buy, it is the best thing for most people to do even in retirement.

Renting or Leasing

As I said previously, your financial situation and your health may determine whether you buy or rent. If you simply do not have the funds to buy or it makes sense to save your money and only rent, there are lots of options today.

If you rent or lease a property, you will not be responsible for paying taxes and insurance. You must know, however, the cost for these are included in your rent. Your landlord is charging you enough rent to cover these expenses also. So, in essence, you are paying taxes and insurance. You just don't have to physically write the check or be responsible to the tax office for the payment.

Your only responsibility will be to pay your rent and any utilities you are responsible for. The landlord will do any repairs and that is a blessing to many people. Some retirees just cannot do repairs and do not want to worry about hiring someone to do repairs. Simple maintenance like painting or caulking is too hard for some people. Removing leaves from a rain gutter, staining a deck, fixing a door hinge, or replacing carpet may be more than you can do. Knowing a landlord is responsible for these things can bring peace of mind too.

When you rent or lease, you have the option of moving whenever you want or if the landlord is not performing well, you can find another place to live. The trouble comes when you like your place, but the landlord fails in his duties. You must live with the problems or move. Moving can be expensive as well.

Having the ability to move whenever you choose is a plus compared to having to sell before you move. Selling a home in order to move can take some time and is a big job. So renting brings flexibility.

Rental properties are often grouped together with other rental properties. Neighbors may move often, which makes the neighborhood a little less stable, but you may have more opportunity to meet new people. If you do not socialize much, this may not even be a consideration for you, but if you socialize, this might be a good thing.

Renting can be by the month, also called a month to month rental agreement. Leasing is usually for at least one year. A long term lease could go for several years. Most landlords will want to renew the lease after a year, so they have the option of raising the rent. If you owned your home, even with a fixed rate mortgage, your monthly payment would not rise. The possibility of rising rent is something to carefully consider when deciding whether to buy or rent.

If you are not familiar with rental agreements or leases, get a copy of any agreement or contract and study it before you sign it. You might also want your attorney to look at it before you sign it. Today, most forms are promulgated by the real estate commission in your state, but not all states have the same laws or forms. Don't assume anything.

I have looked at lots of forms and listened to clients complain they did not know a particular item was in the form before they signed. Once it is signed, you are locked into the agreement for the time period you agreed to. Read every word!

For seniors, I would point out some important parts might be the restrictions on pets. Also, any changes you might want to make like putting up a temporary fence. Or, how about a ramp, in case, you need a wheelchair at some point? Grab rails in the shower are sometimes necessary. Is your parking space saved only for you? These are a few important considerations you should have written into the lease.

Your health and your age will be a determining factor in your decision to rent or buy. Renting offers more flexibility, but buying offers more stability.

Even if you are a senior already, there may still be several moves in your future. There may also be several downsizes in your future. Moving from a large home to a smaller home will require one downsize. Moving from a small home to an apartment or condo could require another downsize.   Only you can determine what is best for your situation, but there are many people that can help give ideas to make the decision making easier. Don't hesitate to call the professionals for help.

Does the Market Matter? *Real estate markets change rapidly from location to location. Interest rates also change rapidly. You should watch both of these to help determine when the best time is to make a move. A one percent difference in interest means a lot in a house payment. A seller's market verses a buyer's market can make a difference as well. Choose the time and the location of your move wisely. It will free up more money for a better retirement.*

Chapter 8

Safety First

Everyone has heard the old saying "Safety First". There are many old sayings concerning safety like, "Safety saves sickness, suffering, sadness" quoted in the early 1900s.

Or "Safety First, Safety Always" by Charles M. Hayes. "Safety is a cheap and effective insurance policy", author unknown.

In the early 1900s there was also "Safety first-today: It may be too late tomorrow." A proverb says, "Better a thousand times careful than once dead."

"We can't be too careful," I used to stress to my family. My mother used to say Benjamin Franklin's quote, "An ounce of prevention is worth a pound of cure." Ask anyone who has fallen and broken a limb how true that one is! The key to a long, healthy life is not to fall!

In Chapter 4, Location was mentioned as the number one consideration for seniors purchasing a new home. One reason location is so important is Safety. Let's look at different kinds of safety. Neighborhoods, cities, outside your home, in your garage, in your yard, and inside the home, different rooms, are all places where safety needs to be considered before there are accidents or mishaps.

Seniors often feel they have lost some physical strength they once possessed. Some know, mentally, they could be slowing down. Even eyesight and dexterity is not what it once was. This can make a person feel vulnerable in certain situations, and I know of instances where some seniors refuse to socialize because of these physical changes that are taking place.

Don't let this be you. Stay in the game! But Be Careful! Let's look at ways we can make safety a part of our daily lives. We want to have a long, healthy, quality filled life and the more we practice safety tips, the better we are.

Safe Neighborhoods- Everyone wants to live in a safe neighborhood. When you are out looking at properties with a real estate agent, you might ask, "Is this a safe neighborhood?" How can the real estate agent answer such a question? Agents cannot discriminate and answering a question like this could be considered discrimination. So, normally the agent will tell you to look up websites in the city or county and find out how many crimes have been committed in that particular area in a particular time period. This is the best way to determine if crime is a problem in that neighborhood.

Another way, is to spend time visiting the neighbors. People love to gossip about the neighborhood and you can learn all kinds of things from the neighbors. Call the Sheriff or local police departments if you still have questions. Go visit the neighborhood in the late evening. See what is going on before you buy. You should do the research, do not rely on others for something as important as this.

Crime in a neighborhood is the biggest deterrent to buying. Sometimes, crimes are committed by one person or one family, and it brings down the value of a home in that neighborhood considerably. Constant crime is not something seniors want to worry about. I have a friend that lives in a nice neighborhood, but the family next door has a grown son that lives with them. That son is constantly stealing items from the neighbors. He has been caught several times but rarely goes to jail. When he does, it is only a short time and he is back doing the same things again. She would like to move, but that is not an option for her at the moment.

You should be able to have peace of mind in retirement. Petty crimes or violent crimes will take your peace away. Location is number one!

Know where the police station is and how long it will take for someone to get to you when you are considering buying a new home. Visit the station; let them know who you are and how many people will be living there if you buy in the area. Give them your phone number in case of emergency.

When you move out of an area, it may be best to change your phone number. If you call 9-1-1 from your cell phone, the call will be directed to the nearest communications center for the area code and prefix of your phone number instead of where you are now located. Calling from home on a land line, your home address is displayed, but not on a cell phone.

Where is the fire station? Where is the EMS? All these services may be needed at some point in your life. Knowing how far away they are and how long it will take to get to you is important in deciding what location is best for your new home.

Be sure to vote for funding of these services in your area. Some smaller towns have a lack of funding which impairs their ability in serving the residents. It is important to seniors that these services are provided.

Outside The Home-There are many places outside the home and in the garage that need to be looked at for safety sake. First, let's consider a burglar trying to break into your home or garage. Locks are the best deterrent. Doors and windows should have good safety locks. Doors should have a key lock and a deadbolt. Windows should have working locks.

Planting thorny bushes below your windows can keep some people away. Lights are also extremely good at deterring theft. A well-lit home on the outside is not as inviting as a dark house. Motion detector lights strategically placed are a big deterrent.

Many people use cameras on their property today. Some are placed on the corners of the home and some burglars will not come on a property if they see a camera on the porch. Doorbells also have cameras in them today. All these things deter crime. Crime is everywhere today, some places are more prevalent than others but crime can occur anywhere. Deterring it before it happens is wise.

If you plan on being gone, stop your newspaper and mail. This is a sign to a thief you are not home. It is easy pickings. Keep your yard mowed and trimmed even when you are away.

My friend has a large doghouse is her backyard with a few chewed dog toys. My friend does not own a dog but a would-be thief might think the dog, a large dog, is inside the house when it is not seen outside. Deterrents can bring a little more safety and peace of mind.

What else is a safety concern? **Accidents.** Accidents can happen anywhere. Falling is an accident every senior needs to think about. A fall can cripple an otherwise healthy person. A fall can be detrimental to your whole health. Preventing a fall can be easier if you take a good look at the potential hazards in your home, in your yard, and in your garage.

Is there a water hose outside in the yard that is not rolled up? This is a potential hazard. Is there a step on the deck or porch that is sticking up higher than the other boards? This is another potential hazard. Is there anything hanging over a walkway that could catch and bring you down? A good look around your property could save a major accident. Fix the little things that are wrong and you will be safer.

Lots of people fall on slippery sidewalks and steps. Is there a way to make them less slippery? Are there handrails? If you have trouble walking, is it time to put in a ramp? Ramps are easier to navigate and a necessity if you are ever in a wheelchair. When looking at purchasing a new home, consider where you could put a ramp if you needed one in the future.

Never walk outside in house shoes. Wear hard-soled shoes outdoors. My mom did this one day and her shoe got caught on a small, fallen tree branch. It caused her to stumble and fall. She broke her shoulder and went through months of agony. She was never able to drive again.

Make a habit of being organized. Put tools away when not in use. Remember, Safety First. Make room to easily navigate your yard and your garage. Too much stuff in the way causes accidents.

Replace plugs when they get broken. Throw away things that have frayed electrical cords. Do not take chances with your safety. Seniors be wise. We cannot do all the things we used to do in the same way. Don't overexert or you will pay for it. Accidents usually happen when people are tired.

Inside The Home -How can we make the inside of our homes safer? We will start with locks on doors and windows. Then, lighting the inside of the home just like the outside is a big deterrent. Light scares away most burglars. You can use timers on lamps and lights when you are away from home to make people think someone is there. Burglars do not want to rob a home when people are present, usually.

Cameras can also be used inside the home. Security companies offer whole home security systems that are monitored twenty-four hours a day. These services can be expensive and there is a monthly fee also.

Individual home cameras also have an alert that is sent to your cell phone if this works for you. It is much less expensive. You can buy cameras online or at any store that sells electronic equipment. They are easy to install by yourself. Cameras work well and if they do not deter the crime, sometimes the criminal is caught because they were first caught on camera.

Curtains, drapes, and shades will keep people from seeing inside. This is cheap protection. Some homeowners are armed, and this is becoming a more popular means of protection even for seniors.

Having your phone nearby at all times is one way to get help. Always know where your phone is. I have the Sheriff's office number in my favorites. 9-1-1 is the first call I would make, however.

Accidents happen inside the home faster than outside the home. There are so many things inside we can trip over. Overcrowded areas are the reason for lots of falls. Make your pathways clear of clutter.

Watch out for pets. Stepping over a sleeping animal, or an animal that is running through the home, can be the cause of many falls for seniors. Put pet beds away from the corners of tables. If you lose your balance while petting your pet, you do not want to fall and hit your head on the corner of a table. Look at your rooms and strategically place your things for added safety.

The bathtub is a big problem for some of us that have stiff muscles or arthritis. Getting in and out is hard. Falling in the tub is one of the easiest ways for us to get hurt. Putting up grab bars in the bathroom is a great idea. Using non-skid mats in the tubs might help. Make sure bathroom rugs do not move when you stand on them.

Home appliances can cause accidents as well. Keep your focused attention when using appliances or anything that can hurt you. An emergency alert necklace might be the answer for you, if you are elderly or in bad health and you live alone.

Pressing the button will alert someone and they can call emergency services and family members.

Practicing **"Safety First"** will bring peace of mind and make your life better. If you are in good health, life is always better. If you are not afraid of living in your home, life is better. If you are not concerned with leaving and going on a trip, that kind of peace of mind brings happiness.

Like Benjamin Franklin said, "An ounce of prevention is worth a pound of cure!"

Chapter 9

Furnishings and Treasures

What To Do With Them

Many say, "Moving is never fun! It is something we have to do from time to time." Downsizing and moving to a smaller home because of age or health issues is one of those times when it becomes necessary. To make it easier, you will need to remove the clutter from your home. You may have accumulated many things in your long life. You look around and try to imagine what you could live without.

Then, you sit down and say, "I can't do this!"

"Yes, you can!"

There are many things in your home you can live without and you will not even miss most of them when they are gone. Surely, you have some collections or souvenirs you will want to share with your children or friends. Go ahead and give them away. There will also be decorative items that won't fit in the new place. Clean these out and the task is already lighter.

I have seen lots of collections in my real estate career. They range from dolls to figurines to almost anything. I've seen thimbles, cups, knives, candles and candleholders, arrow heads, flags, guns, books, shot glasses, vases, and even tools. Antiques come in all kinds, shapes and sizes.

On a personal note, my dear, sweet aunt had a lot of collections, art pieces, many of which she made or painted. My aunt was quite the artist! As she got older, she realized the need to move closer to family.

The city she lived in had grown considerably with time. It was no longer the quaint hometown she enjoyed as a young woman. It was now a dynamic and fast-paced, larger city in Texas. The traffic was busy day and night.

My aunt's driving skills began to suffer. She was no longer the fastest driver on the road. As the highways became wider and more lanes were added, the less my aunt drove. Soon, there came a time when just going to a doctor's appointment was a big deal. The timing had to be just right. High traffic times on the roads determined her daily schedule.

She really needed to make a move. The big question was what to do with all her things. There were many things in her home she treasured. Some were antiques passed down from family members long gone. She had no children to give these items to, and that made the task even greater. There were many paintings and china paintings she had created throughout the years.

I offered to help her in any way I could. I came up with all kinds of ideas. She was tired and her health was failing. She could not bring herself to allow someone else to come in and handle the packing, the dissemination of some of her things, and the entire move. My aunt was a strong woman and had always been in control. Allowing someone else to make decisions was not something she would do.

It was never convenient for her, and she made one excuse after the other. She stayed in her home for several more years. She refused to make the decisions she knew she needed to make.

Yes, it is hard to give away or sell things you treasure. If you do not do this while you are able, someone else will have to do it for you later.

My aunt thought the project of moving was too much. She stayed in her home as long as she could. When her health deteriorated to the point of needing full-time care, she moved into a nursing home. She was only there for a very short time.

Yes, I had the job of taking care of her things. It was not easy. I gave away what I thought she would like to have given to the people in her life. I donated many things to charities. I hired help because she had a large house filled to the brim with all kinds of things. Household furnishings, dishes, furniture, food, and appliances went to various locations. The collections, artwork, jewelry, and more valuable treasures had to find homes too. It was a big job. It took a long time.

It could be the same way with your home and your things. If you downsize a little at a time, the job is broken up in increments and does not become such a major problem. My advice is, "Do it now!"

Do it while you are in good health. Make the decisions yourself about what happens to your things. Don't put that task on someone else's shoulders.

Maybe you have a pretty plate someone special gave to you on a special occasion and you have thought about how the neighbor next door has admired it for years. Why not give it to her now and see her surprise? What a nice gesture it would be to make your friendship even stronger. If you have no special plans for that plate after you are gone, give it to a friend now. You will still be able to admire it at her house.

Once you have done the initial run through of your 'treasures' and especially the ones with sentimental value, decide what to keep and what not to keep. Remove them either by giving them away or packing them up for the move. Now, it is time to find a place for all the other things.

You can take your things to a consignment shop or rent a booth in an antique mall and slowly sell each piece one at a time. If you have years to downsize and you want a good price for each item, this might work for you. Renting a booth in an antique mall can also be fun. I have done this before, but it proved to be a lot of work. This can take a long time. Most people do not have this much time or patience. The booth rental fees can eat up your profit as well. I really never made that much more doing it this way than choosing an easier option.

You might call an antique dealer and get one price for a whole group. Expect them to offer a low price as they want to make a profit on the resale. It is much easier though, and more convenient for a dealer to come and haul away a lot of stuff quickly.

Estate sales are like garage sales but more things are usually offered and the prices are higher. There are companies that will come arrange, price, advertise and sell your things in your home for a fee. Fees vary but average about forty percent. Well known estate dealers do get more money for your things and the forty percent does not hurt as bad if they get a higher price for that old corner chair and your other treasures.

I have had clients that hired estate dealers to sell their things. Most of my clients were happy with the results. Some areas do not have estate dealers. I lived and worked in a retirement area where there were several dealers.

The dealers will inventory all your things and you can be involved in the pricing. When the day of the sale comes, the owner usually leaves the premises. Sometimes, it is too emotional to watch your things being sold. The owners come back after the sale and the inventory is done again for anything that did not sell. The owner is given a check that day.

If you hire an estate dealer, the first step will be to appraise and price the items you wish to sell. Second, the items must be prepared for sale. This can mean cleaning or repairing some things. Arranging and displaying is important to get the highest price possible.

As I mentioned before, advertising will determine how many buyers come to your sale. Don't skimp on advertising. An estate dealer with a following of buyers brings interest to your sale. So, hire a dealer with a good reputation and following.

The estate dealer's employees will run the sale. If there are items that do not sell, the dealer will handle donations to charities for you.

The dealer cleans up and removes the signs, and the owner can go forth with their new plans. Sometimes, there is an extra fee for the cleanup. Make sure you discuss this before you hire an estate sale company. This is one of the easiest ways to sell your furnishings.

Auctions are also an option. It works about the same way as an estate sale. Auctions can usually draw a larger crowd, but that depends on your location. Auctioneer fees also vary. If you use an auctioneer, use someone you know or get lots of references. Ask people who have hired an auctioneer to dispose of their goods about their experiences. Ask several people to make sure this is the way you want to proceed. Find out if the auctioneer you are thinking of using is good at advertising and doing all the paperwork involved. Auctions happen so quickly, everything must be written down. Full accounting is very important.

Research auctioneers online. My state has a licensing agency for auctioneers and the website advertises auctions statewide. This is a very convenient way to sell your items because so many people like to go to auctions and buy things. Real estate sold by auction is becoming more popular especially in rural areas where buyers are few and far between. An auction can be a fast way and a profitable way to dispose of your goods.

Do your research and don't just pick the first auctioneer or estate dealer you find. You want to get as much money as you can for the things you want to sell. Be wise; don't think your items are made of gold unless they are! Most people think their things are worth more than they are because they have sentimental value. This is the reason to hire a professional that can help you reasonably price your things. After all, the goal is to sell!

No matter which way you choose to dispose of your treasures, it will feel good afterwards. Yes, you may be hesitant at first, thinking you cannot get rid of certain things because of the sentimental value you have placed on them. Remember, someone else will be able to enjoy them now. Think of it in that way and it is easier to let go. The extra money you put in your pocket will help the pain too.

Downsizing your things will make your life easier.

Here's a good way to get started!

Hiring an individual or a company to sell your things is wise. But even with the extra help, you will be making lots of decisions. I have done this for myself and others many times and I think a good way to get started is to have four corners of a room designated for different items.

In corner 1, you can put all the things you want to keep. This will include the items you use every day plus special things like photo albums or those with special meaning attached.

In corner 2, place all the things you want to give away to the special people in your life. You may not have decided who you want to give these things to yet or when, but put them here. You can make those decisions later. We are just separating for now. It will give you a better picture of where you want to go and how to get there.

In corner 3, place the things you know right now you want to sell. This will also help you decide which way to sell your items. If you do not have enough items, some estate sale dealers or auctioneers are not willing to work with you. You may have to find other ways to sell your things. By now, things are getting clearer. You have lost nothing at this point, but you are looking at things with a more objective point of view. If you are terribly sentimental like me, sorting like this helps a lot.

In corner 4, place the things you want to donate. You may know some items will not sell. Maybe some things have been used for too long but still have good use left in them and someone else might appreciate them. Donate all you can. Throw away the rest.

Once, your furnishings have been downsized,

It is time to sell the house.

Now, stage your home with fewer furnishings for more money!

Downsizing furnishings can be done without selling your house, if the time is not right for a smaller home. Downsizing furnishings more than once can make a very big job easier. I have downsized my furnishings several times already. Twice I downsized into a smaller home but other times I did not. Downsizing is different for different people. I have had several businesses in my life, traveled a lot, and accumulated lots of furnishings.

Downsizing only once may be what you need. On the other hand, you may be like me and have too much of everything. A multi-step approach may work better.

Chapter 10

How to Choose the Right Agent

Selling your home:

How do you choose the right real estate agent to sell your larger home and buy another smaller home? Aren't all real estate agents the same?

Over my forty year career, I have heard all kinds of ideas and arguments about how to choose a real estate agent. I have listed many homes and many times I have interviewed sellers and they have interviewed me. I have seen many people list their homes for sale with a relative or friend. I have also not been chosen to represent my relatives and friends more than once.

As an agent, you feel disappointed and sometimes even heartbroken when a relative chooses an agent from your association over you. Your relative or friend may be very close and you expected them to choose you but they did not. Why, you ask yourself?

"I thought they liked me," you bemoan. Don't get your feelings hurt. Sometimes, people don't want you to know their personal business. Other times, the other agent made a better listing presentation than you did. Agents, I'm talking to you now. You know what I am saying is true. Business is business.

Sellers, let's talk about the listing decision. Yes, you have a decision to make. I have seen many sellers in the past, hire the first real estate agent they called to view their property or maybe, give a free market analysis. Some sellers hire any relative or good friend that has a real estate license. Sellers, you have choices. Today's informed sellers know they can call several agents and interview them for the job. Yes, listing your home for sale is a job. If you were a store owner and needed a salesman, you would certainly interview more than one salesperson for a job you wanted to fill. Shouldn't it be the same way when you are listing your home for sale?

Your home could be the largest investment you have. Trusting the sale to go smoothly and quickly will depend upon the person you hire to market and sell your home.

The agent you hire works for you and you call the shots. Part of the fiduciary relationship, as we have talked about earlier in Chapter 4, requires the agent to follow your instructions. However, they are the ones that have the knowledge, so it is a two-way street. They listen to you and you listen to them. If you had the knowledge they have, you would not need them. So listen to their recommendations.

The agent you hire should be knowledgeable about your neighborhood, your city, your county. They should know the market conditions at the present time and the direction the market is headed. Knowing these details will help you and your agent determine a good price for your property.

The agent should also be able to help you stage your home. They should be able to recommend changes you should make before you place it on the market. First impressions are most important. Do not list your home before you make the necessary changes. Buyers look once and rarely come back after improvements are made. So have your home ready for show, the moment it goes on the MLS, multiple listing service.

Real estate agents often specialize in various areas of the real estate industry. Some agents act only as seller agents and some as buyer agents. Others will act for both buyers and sellers. Many have special designations or certifications showing they have attended or graduated from special classes and have more specific knowledge regarding one aspect of the industry.

Should you look for someone who works with seniors? There are designations for different things. The SRES® designation stands for Seniors Real Estate Specialist. There are designations for buyer agents like me. The ABR® designation, Accredited Buyer Representative, says I am an experienced and well qualified buyer agent. The SRS, Seller Representative Specialist, brings the agent to a greater depth of seller advocacy. Choosing an agent with designations can sometimes help you know the agent has the knowledge to perform their duties at a higher level of competency but not always. Having the knowledge is important but putting it into action is another thing.

I was at a training class one time, and I met a very nice lady during lunch. We sat together and conversed during our break. She told me about her designations and I was astounded. She had over 15 designations and certifications. She had been in the real estate business for 9 years. Her husband was a businessman and gone a lot of the time. She was middle-aged and their children were grown and gone from home. She took up real estate like a hobby.

She enjoyed going to classes and therefore had received many designations. As we talked, I explained I owned and operated my own office. I had 17 agents working for me at the time. She inquired if I might be interested in hiring her.

So, I began to ask her more questions about her experience. I almost fell out of my chair when she told me she had never sold a house. Not one! She had never worked with a client and did not even know how to get started.

I wondered, "What kind of broker did she have?" I would have no one like this on my team. I would have trained her the moment she came to work for me. Not all brokers are the same, and they do not always supervise their agents.

If you are hiring an agent, their success is usually tied to the success of their broker. So, don't just look at the agent. Look at the office they work for and the broker that is supposed to supervise them. If this is not a good situation, pass on that agent. The broker has the last say in every transaction and should be watching what the agent is doing. Most of the time these days, this is not the case. We have lots of runaway agents working without good supervision.

When listing your home, ask questions. Ask lots of questions. Ask how many transactions the agent has had in the past 12 months. How many were seller sides and how many were buyer sides? Ask if they had both sides. Ask how many transactions occurred in the MLS and where the agent rates on the list. This will give you a good idea if they are a top producer or not.

Top producers may not always be your best choice. Top producers are very busy and may not spend enough time with you if you need extra help in staging or extra time with explanations of contracts. However, top producers know how to get homes sold quickly. You want an agent who will get you the most money, in the shortest amount of time, with the least inconvenience to you. This may or may not be a top producer in your area. Look at everything involved in your transaction.

Every transaction is different and requires different marketing ideas. A good agent will have good marketing skills. Advertising will be their greatest asset. The more buyers looking at your home usually results in the largest offers.

Your selling price is determined by the square footage, the condition, and the average market price of homes similar to yours. You want to be competitive in your pricing. You will also take into account how quickly you need to sell.

Curb appeal is everything. If your home doesn't say "Come on in," it could be on the market for a long time. Make sure you make the outside as appealing as possible.

The next thing to determine about the agent you hire is their proficiency at negotiation. Negotiation is where you make money or lose money. An agent needs to be able to negotiate on your behalf. They have to have good working relationships with other agents in your area but they must represent you first, not just appease other agents. They also must be willing to be flexible to make the deal happen, just like you must be flexible. They must negotiate and negotiate to get you the best deal possible. Busy agents must take the time necessary to negotiate not just take the first offer that comes along.

The negotiation process is where having a seller's agent that represents you is most important. Some people like to sell their homes by themselves, for sale by owners. It is impossible to negotiate with a buyer and get the best price if you do not have that third party representing you. Stay away from the buyers or you will lose your leverage.

Buying your next home:

As I talked in Chapter 4 about buyer representation, choosing the right agent to represent you is imperative if you want a good deal. If you are moving to a new home in the same area as the one you just sold, you might use the same agent that sold your home. This is not always wise, however.

The agent should have knowledge and experience in buyer representation. You can and should interview agents for buyer representation just like you interviewed agents to sell your home. You should get a signed contract for buyer representation just like the listing contract you signed to sell. Different states have different ways of handling buyer representation. I am most familiar with Texas, so if you are in another state, it may differ.

The agent's duties and responsibilities will be outlined in the contract. You may have to pay for this representation out of your pocket or it may be paid by the seller of the home you decide to purchase. Either way, the cost of personal buyer representation is well worth the cost.

A buyer's agent will be watching for problems in the new home, will be examining the inspector's reports, going over the title commitment, and negotiating and explaining contracts to you. Buyer agents represent you, not individual homes or seller's interests.

As discussed in Chapter 4, confidentiality is part of the fiduciary relationship. You should be able to talk freely to your buyer's agent about your home needs, your financial situation, your likes and dislikes. Your buyer agent should not breach any part of the fiduciary relationship.

Disclosure is another part that could mean money in your pocket. The buyer's agent must disclose anything they know about a property you are interested in. Knowing personal details about why a seller is selling and their timeframe could give you an advantage over other buyers. If you knew how many other offers the seller had over a period of time, couldn't this be an advantage also? These are just a few things your buyer agent may bring to the table.

Some state laws vary in buyer representation and in some states it is not taught like in other states. You may be in one of these states where the agent represents both parties to a transaction. The agent may not know what you are talking about when you ask for buyer representation. In cases like this, be sure to keep your business to yourself. If confidentiality and disclosure is not practiced, don't make statements you don't want the seller to know.

If you are moving a long distance away from your previous residence, it is hard to know who the best agent is in a new area. Sometimes, your listing agent can refer you to someone in the new location. Agents know other agents across the country from networking opportunities or online networks they belong to. Finding an Accredited Buyer Representative, ABR® may be your best choice. You can meet over the phone or online before you arrive at the new place.

If you are moving to a new area of the country you are not familiar with, you will need to look at more homes than usually necessary to find the perfect spot. You will have lots of questions about the city, the county, the shopping, the recreation opportunities, the schools, the churches, the city government, and so much more. A good buyer's agent will be patient with you and answer all your questions.

When I was serving clients that came from another area, I would take time to tour them through the city and explain routes and intersections we were driving. I would point out good shopping places, schools, and restaurants. I would show several homes and then I would drive my clients around giving them a good idea of what was available in our community. Showing them things I thought they might be interested in knowing, relieved some of the tension of home shopping. Then, we would look at a few more homes.

Educating my buyers on the area, as we also looked at properties, made them feel more comfortable in their buying decision.

A happy buyer will usually call you when they get ready to sell and downsize again. Word of mouth advertising is the best kind. A good referral from a pleased client goes a long way.

So, when you are looking for a buyer agent to represent you, ask your friends about the agents they have used. Ask the hard questions about the agent. Not just questions about how nice they were, but questions about how many showings they had, how long it took to find a home, the amount of negotiating that was needed, the competency of the agent, how quick they returned phone calls, and overall satisfaction.

Communication is the key to a successful and pleasant transaction. If you call your agent, and they do not return the call quickly or at all, you need a different agent. Don't accept the answer, they were busy. Are they too busy to take care of you, their client or potential client? If they will not call or text you back, they will also neglect other agents' calls and texts to show property or to negotiate a contract.

The difference between agents is like night and day. If you have bought and sold homes in the past, you already know this. I have worked in small towns and large cities. I find different levels of agents in both.

The lengths that some agents go to these days is amazing to me; some good, some bad. When I started in the business in 1978, there were several brokers in our town that were known to do shady deals and we avoided deals with them when we could. When one of them called and wanted to show our listing, we held our breath hoping their buyer would not be interested. We knew the contract would come half-filled in and with errors. We knew we would have multiple discussions that would eventually become heated. We knew we would have to fight tooth and nail to protect our clients.

Not all agents are the same, some are just licensees (a licensee is anyone that has a license), but some have the designation as REALTORS®. **What is the difference?**

REALTORS® are held to a higher standard. Realtors® join a local, state, and the National Association of Realtors®. They pledge to abide by the **Code of Ethics and Standards of Practice**. If you search REALTORS® Code of Ethics, you will find a National Association of Realtors website where you can read the Code of Ethics which has been in existence for over 100 years, and Standards of Practice which is updated periodically. Realtors® regularly take classes on the Code of

Ethics and Standards of Practice as part of their continuing education. They pledge to abide by these rules when they are accepted into membership. All Realtors® belong to a local, state, and the National Association of Realtors®, that allows them to call themselves Realtors®, which is a trademark name. Licensees that are not Realtors® are not held to such high standards.

The Standards of Practice was updated in January 2020 and Article 1-7 has been amended to include: Upon receiving a request in writing from a cooperating broker, who submits an offer to the listing broker, the listing broker shall provide, a written affirmation to the cooperating broker, as soon as possible, stating that the offer has been submitted to the seller, or a written notification that the seller has waived the obligation to have the offer presented. This article covers rental property transactions as well.

This wording can be very important to a seller or a buyer. Realtors® must abide by these Ethics and Practices but a licensee is not under such obligation. Choosing a Realtor® is the better choice. This is only one such example. Check out Article 1-3 and Article 1-15 also.

Article 1-3 states that Realtor® shall not deliberately mislead the owner as to the market value of a property in order to secure the listing. This is good information for people needing to sell a home.

Article 1-15 was amended in 2009. It says a Realtor®, with written permission from seller will disclose any other offers and where the other offers came from, such as the listing agent, the listing office, or another cooperating broker. This is valuable information for a buyer client.

The laws are stricter today and more complicated. There is a big difference in licensees and Realtors®. Take time to read the Code of Ethics and Standards of Practice and choose an agent that is knowledgeable about these and holds themselves to a higher standard.

Ask your agent to go over a blank contract form with you before you want to purchase. You need to know what choices you have in a contract. *Your buyer's agent will help you get the best deal and the most amenities for your budget. Your agent is on your side and the more they know about your needs and preferences the better they can serve you*. Your transaction will go smoother when you have a great working relationship with your buyer agent. So, spend some time getting to know your agent and choose the right one for you. Don't just accept the first one, or one that is a relative or friend. Interview a buyer's agent like you would interview a seller's agent.

I have gone into depth in choosing the right agent. Hopefully, this will help you get the best deals when selling, and buying your new retirement home!

Chapter 11

Are You Ready

To Make The Move?

Have you been considering making the move for some time? Or is the idea new to you? Either way, there are many things to think about and plans to make. A well-organized move takes good planning but the extra time you will spend planning and organizing will be worth it in the end.

Some people have moved many times during their lives but others have only moved a few times. Knowing how to move makes it easier. I have moved many times. I am experienced in packing and unpacking. I pack everything that I am not going to be using ahead of time. I label all my boxes with a permanent marker. Don't fail to label the boxes! So easy to do yet many people forget to do it, and later finding something you need is a nightmare.

Downsizing a little at a time is a good idea. When you get ready to move into a smaller home that is easier to maintain, the packing will be easier if you have already begun the downsizing. Most people have TOO MUCH STUFF! We can live without all the stuff as you will find out as you start this process of downsizing.

When you finally decide to move, and you have made the decisions about what kind of home you need, what amenities you want in the new home and have chosen a mortgage company and officer, been pre-approved for your loan, it is time to find the perfect Realtor®.

It is all a process. Step by step you will get it done. Planning and organization will make this job easier. The professionals you choose to work with will help you fill in all the details.

Once a home is located, the deadlines begin. Be ready. This is where all the previous planning, packing, organizing, comes in handy. Deadlines put pressure on everyone and mistakes can happen when things are rushed. There will be many decisions to make in a hurry. This is why I have tried to prepare you. The more you know now, the better.

Contract offers have deadlines. Option periods are deadlines. Repairs in a contract are under a deadline. Even getting your loan approved is a deadline. Loan pre-approval is not loan approval. Loan approval does not happen until all the paperwork is done and an underwriter says it is approved and the funds have been made available to the title company to close. There are deadlines and more deadlines. All this happens in a relatively short period of time. This is why having all your documentation ready to give to the loan officer before you find the new home is best.

Do not pack up your important papers before you have given everything to your loan officer. Make sure those boxes are labeled as well. You may have to dig into them again before it is all done.

After closing, the move begins. Hire some help. Seniors need to save money but more than that we need to save our bodies. Do not overdo or you will pay for it many times over.

I have hurt myself so many times, thinking I can still do that! Can you relate?

Moving companies charge in various ways. Some charge by the box and some charge by weight. Some charge by cubic feet and by the mile. It all depends on how far away you are moving as to what methods you might want to incorporate in your move. Today, you can rent a truck or trailer or even a POD. You pack it up and the company comes to get it and deliver it to your new home.

I personally prefer to pack my things myself. There are certain things that have more value to me and I want to make sure they are packed correctly. Big items and furniture is something I don't mind paying for help to move. I only have a little of the strength I used to have and I prefer to save it for the smaller items I can move by myself.

When the whole process is over, you can put your feet up and say, "Well done." It seems like a lot to do, but in the end it is well worth it. Living in a smaller home with only a portion of the 'Stuff' you used to have to dust and care for is a blessing. You will have more time to do the things you want to do, and maybe, more money to spend. Maintaining a large home and yard is expensive. Why not use that money for a trip or a new wardrobe?

These are the 'Golden Years'. Make them memorable. Enjoy your life and don't be afraid to try new things. Meet new friends and go places you have never been before. This can be the time of your life!

Downsizing is for everyone over the age of 50, I used to say. But, my millennial friend says it is also for people younger than age 50. She falls in the Generation Y.2 category. Why not shed some clutter and downsize into a smaller home if the children have grown up and gone? It is time for more leisure, and keeping up with the Jones' went out of style a long time ago.

Tiny homes are the new thing. Grandma houses in backyards are even becoming popular today. Smaller homes, condos, apartments, manufactured homes, the choice is yours. Retirement homes come in all sizes and places. Let your imagination run wild, and explore what your market has to offer. You may be surprised.

It is a good time to Downsize!

Author's Notes and Acknowledgments

My thanks to all who have contributed to this book; my family, friends, colleagues, clients and especially Loan Originator Tony Stevenson for his input on loan products and processes, my friends Denise and Nancy who gave personal insight in their personal downsizing.

I do not receive referral fees from service providers and strongly urge my readers to thoroughly research any suggestions I make. Every transaction in real estate is different and requires different solutions. My training and experience as a Texas real estate broker and Realtor® is shared for informational purposes only. Please consult your local realty professionals for agent representation, and only attorneys for legal advice.

I enjoy helping others learn practical steps to enhance their lives. If this book has helped you, please take a moment and review it on Amazon or Goodreads. I appreciate your thoughts and kindness.

My next book will be coming out soon. Please follow me and enjoy my next work on Amazon or Goodreads. Thank You.

www.ingramcontent.com/pod-product-compliance
Lightning Source LLC
Chambersburg PA
CBHW071406210526
45465CB00001B/281